ABITUR-TRAINING

Englisch – Grammatikübungen

Rainer Jacob

Mit Lernvideos

STARK

Autor

Rainer Jacob hat durch seine Arbeit in der Lehrerfortbildung, der Lehrplankommission sowie als Studiendirektor und Fachberater für das Fach Englisch sehr viel praxisnahe Lehrerfahrung vorzuweisen. Er veröffentlichte im STARK Verlag bereits zahlreiche Bücher und Unterrichtsbeiträge für das Fach Englisch.

Vom selben Autor sind im STARK Verlag u. a. die folgenden Titel erschienen:
- Training Grundwissen Englisch – Übertritt in die Oberstufe
- Abitur-Training Englisch – Themenwortschatz
- Abitur-Wissen Englisch – Landeskunde Großbritannien
- Abitur-Wissen Englisch – Landeskunde USA

© 2016 Stark Verlag GmbH
www.stark-verlag.de
1. Auflage 1994

Inhalt

Vorwort

Das Adverb • The Adverb 1

1   Form und Bildung 1
1.1 Ableitung vom Adjektiv 1
1.2 Adjektiv und Adverb mit gleicher Form 1

2   Gebrauch 2

3   Vertiefung 2
3.1 Steigerung 2
3.2 Adverb oder Adjektiv? 2
3.3 Adjektiv und Adverb mit unterschiedlicher Bedeutung 3
3.4 Stellung des Adverbs im Satz 3

4   Übungen 4

Der Artikel • The Article 11

1   Bestimmter Artikel • Definite Article 11

2   Unbestimmter Artikel • Indefinite Article 12

3   Übungen 13

Bedingungssätze • Conditional Sentences 17

1   Form und Bildung 17
1.1 Konditional I • Conditional 17
1.2 Konditional II • Conditional Perfect 17

2   Gebrauch 17

3   Vertiefung 19
3.1 Zeitenfolge • The Sequence of Tenses 19
3.2 Sonderfälle 20

4   Übungen 22

Fortsetzung siehe nächste Seite

Das Gerundium • The Gerund 29

1 Form und Bildung 29

2 Gebrauch 29
2.1 Funktionen des Gerundiums im Satz 29
2.2 Gerundium nach Präpositionen 30

3 Vertiefung 31
3.1 Gerundium in Verbindung mit bestimmten Verben 31
3.2 Gerundium und Infinitiv mit unterschiedlicher Bedeutung 32
3.3 Gerundium mit eigenem Subjekt 33
3.4 Gerundium anstelle eines Adverbialsatzes 34

4 Übungen 34

Modale Hilfsverben • Modal Auxiliaries 41

1 Form und Bildung 41
1.1 Übersicht über die modalen Hilfsverben und ihre Ersatzformen 42
1.2 *can* als Beispiel für ein Modalverb in allen Zeiten 42

2 Gebrauch 43
2.1 *can/could* (‚können‘) – Ersatzverb: *to be able to* 43
2.2 *may/might* (‚dürfen‘) – Ersatzverb: *to be allowed to* 43
2.3 *must* (‚müssen‘) – Ersatzverb: *to have to* 43
2.4 *will/would* (‚wollen‘) – Ersatzverben: *to want, to wish, to desire* 44
2.5 *shall/should* (‚sollen‘) – Ersatzverben: *to be to, to want* 44

3 Vertiefung 44
3.1 *must not/need not* 44
3.2 Deutsches ‚sollen‘ 45

4 Übungen 45

Indirekte Rede • Reported Speech 49

1 Gebrauch 49
1.1 Pronomina • Pronouns 49
1.2 Zeiten 50
1.3 Besonderheiten bei der Zeichensetzung und Übersetzung 50

2 Vertiefung 50
2.1 Zeitenverschiebung • The Backshift of Tenses 50
2.2 Adverbiale 52
2.3 Hilfsverben • Auxiliaries 53

3 Übungen 53

Der Infinitiv • The Infinitive 59

1 Form und Bildung 59
1.1 Aktiv 59
1.2 Passiv 59

2 Gebrauch 59

3 Vertiefung 60
3.1 Infinitiv mit *to* 60
3.2 Infinitiv ohne *to* 61
3.3 Objekt + Infinitiv-Konstruktion 62
3.4 *with* + Infinitiv 62
3.5 *for* + Infinitiv 62
3.6 Infinitiv im Passiv 63
3.7 Deutsches ‚lassen‘ 63

4 Übungen 64

Die Partizipien • The Participles 71

1 Partizip Präsens • Present Participle 71
1.1 Form und Bildung 71
1.2 Gebrauch 71

2 Partizip Perfekt • Past Participle 72
2.1 Form und Bildung 72
2.2 Gebrauch 72

3 Vertiefung 72
3.1 Satzverkürzung • Syntactic Compression 72
3.2 Fehlerquelle: *Misrelated Participles* 74
3.3 *with* + Partizip 75

4 Übungen 76

Das Passiv • The Passive 83

1 Form und Bildung 83
1.1 Einfache Form • Simple Passive 83
1.2 Verlaufsform • Passive Progressive 84

2 Vertiefung 84
2.1 Verben mit direktem Objekt 84
2.2 Verben mit zwei Objekten (mit direktem und indirektem Objekt) ... 85

Fortsetzung siehe nächste Seite

2.3 Verben mit präpositionalem Objekt 85
2.4 Infinitiv Passiv nach Verben des Sagens 86

3 Übungen 86

Präpositionen • Prepositions 95

1 Form 95

2 Gebrauch 96

3 Vertiefung 96
3.1 Hauptfehlerquellen 96
3.2 Typische Wendungen mit Präpositionen 98

4 Übungen 98

Relativpronomen • Relative Pronouns 105

1 Form und Bildung 105

2 Gebrauch 105
2.1 Relativpronomen als Subjekt 105
2.2 Relativpronomen als Objekt 106

3 Vertiefung 106
3.1 Notwendige oder bestimmende Relativsätze
    (defining relative clauses) 106
3.2 Nicht-notwendige oder nicht-bestimmende Relativsätze
    (non-defining relative clauses) 107
3.3 what/which 108

4 Übungen 108

Zeiten • Tenses 113

1 Form und Bildung 113
1.1 Present tense 113
1.2 Future tense 113
1.3 Past tense 113
1.4 Present perfect 113
1.5 Past perfect 114

2 Gebrauch 114
2.1 Present tense 114
2.2 Future tense 115
2.3 Past tense 115

| 2.4 | Present perfect | 116 |
| 2.5 | Past perfect | 117 |

3	Vertiefung	118
3.1	Einfache Form oder Verlaufsform?	118
3.2	Verben ohne Verlaufsform	118
3.3	*always* + Verlaufsform	119
3.4	Simple Past – Present Perfect	119
3.5	*since – for*	121
3.6	Formen des Futurs	121

| 4 | Übungen | 122 |

Tests		129
Test 1: Changing Places		129
Test 2: Homeless Teenagers		131
Test 3: Are You Eating the Right Kind of Food?		134

| Unregelmäßige Verben • Irregular Verbs | | 137 |

| Lösungen • Key | | 141 |

 Im Hinblick auf eine eventuelle Begrenzung des Datenvolumens wird empfohlen, dass Sie sich beim Ansehen der Videos im WLAN befinden. Haben Sie keine Möglichkeit, den QR-Code zu scannen, finden Sie die Lernvideos auch unter:
http://qrcode.stark-verlag.de/82452V

Autor: Rainer Jacob

Vorwort

Liebe Schülerin, lieber Schüler,

dieses Buch kann und will eine herkömmliche Grammatik nicht ersetzen. Es beschäftigt sich vielmehr mit den grammatikalischen Erscheinungen, die auch Oberstufenschülern noch Schwierigkeiten bereiten.

Jedes der zwölf Kapitel dieses Bandes behandelt einen grammatikalischen Schwerpunkt, z. B. das Gerundium, *if*-Sätze oder die Zeiten, um nur einige zu nennen.

Diese Konzeption spiegelt sich auch im Aufbau der einzelnen Kapitel wider.

- Im Allgemeinen wird zu Beginn eines Kapitels die **Bildung** der grammatikalischen Struktur erläutert.
- Im zweiten Teil wird auf deren **Gebrauch** eingegangen.
- Im dritten Abschnitt wird besonders das hervorgehoben, was auch für Oberstufenschüler eine **häufige Fehlerquelle** darstellen kann.
- Im vierten Teil – dem **Übungsteil** – wird das zuvor Erläuterte intensiv an zusammenhängenden Texten und vielfältigen Aufgabenstellungen eingeübt.

Zu einigen grammatischen Strukturen, mit denen erfahrungsgemäß viele Schüler Schwierigkeiten haben, gibt es zusätzlich Lernvideos. An den entsprechenden Stellen im Buch befindet sich ein QR-Code, den Sie mithilfe Ihres Smartphones oder Tablets scannen können – Sie gelangen so schnell und einfach zum zugehörigen Lernvideo.

Am Ende des Bandes finden Sie drei **Tests** mit Texten und Aufgaben. Alle im Buch behandelten grammatikalischen Konstruktionen können hier – durcheinander gewürfelt und gleichsam ohne „Vorwarnung" – noch einmal trainiert werden. Dass es zu allen Aufgaben auch **Lösungen** gibt, versteht sich von selbst.

Der Trainingsband unterstützt Sie nicht nur bei der Wiederholung der Grammatik, sondern hilft Ihnen auch, landeskundliche Themen des Lehrplans aufzufrischen. Jedes Grammatikkapitel behandelt inhaltlich ein prüfungsrelevantes Thema wie *Immigration*, *Environment*, *European Union*, *Media* u. a. So stellt dieses Buch eine optimale Vorbereitung auf Klausuren und Prüfungen im Fach Englisch dar.

Rainer Jacob

Das Adverb · The Adverb

1   Form und Bildung

1.1   Ableitung vom Adjektiv

	Adjektiv		Adverb
Im Normalfall wird an das Adjektiv *-ly* angehängt.	final	→	finally
	immediate	→	immediately
	sincere	→	sincerely
In Sonderfällen			
• wird -y zu -i,	angry	→	angrily
	busy	→	busily
	happy	→	happily
	noisy	→	noisily
Ausnahme:	shy	→	shyly
• fällt -e weg und -ly wird angefügt,	due	→	duly
	true	→	truly
	whole	→	wholly
• fällt -e weg und -y wird angefügt,	comfortable	→	comfortably
	possible	→	possibly
	sensible	→	sensibly
	terrible	→	terribly
• wird -ic zu -ically.	automatic	→	automatically
	scientific	→	scientifically
	systematic	→	systematically
Ausnahmen bilden folgende Adjektive:	friendly	→	in a friendly way
	good	→	well

1.2   Adjektiv und Adverb mit gleicher Form

daily, early, fast, long, low, straight, weekly, yearly etc.

2 Gebrauch

Das Adverb dient zur **näheren Bestimmung** eines

- Verbs,

  Joan <u>sings</u> <u>beautifully</u>.
  Joan <u>singt</u> <u>schön</u>.

- Adjektivs,

  That was <u>really</u> <u>interesting</u>.
  Das war <u>wirklich</u> <u>interessant</u>.

- Adverbs oder

  Jimmy can drive a car <u>extremely</u> <u>well</u>.
  Jimmy kann <u>sehr gut</u> Auto fahren.

- eines ganzen Satzes.

  <u>Fortunately</u>, we were not in the cinema when the fire broke out.
  <u>Glücklicherweise</u> waren wir nicht im Kino, als das Feuer ausbrach.

3 Vertiefung

3.1 Steigerung

Adverbien auf *-ly* werden mit *more* und *most* gesteigert.

Young people should drive <u>more carefully</u>.
Junge Menschen sollten vorsichtiger Auto fahren.

3.2 Adverb oder Adjektiv?

Nach folgenden Verben steht das **Adjektiv** (aber nicht das Adverb):

- *to become, to get, to grow, to keep, to look ('aussehen'), to remain, to seem*

  All the boys <u>remained</u> <u>quiet</u>.
  Alle Jungen blieben still.

- *to smell, to sound, to taste*

  Your cakes always <u>taste</u> <u>delicious</u>.
  Deine Kuchen schmecken immer lecker.

  The new song <u>sounds</u> <u>great</u>.
  Das neue Lied hört sich großartig an.

3.3 Adjektiv und Adverb mit unterschiedlicher Bedeutung

Adjektiv		Adverb		Adjektiv		Adverb	
fair	= gerecht	fairly	= ziemlich	just	= gerade	justly	= zu Recht
hard	= schwer	hardly	= kaum	near	= nahe	nearly	= beinahe
high	= hoch	highly	= sehr	late	= spät	lately	= in letzter Zeit, kürzlich

3.4 Stellung des Adverbs im Satz

Adverbien können an folgenden Positionen im Satz stehen:

- am Anfang (*front-position*)

  In 20 years the number of youths arrested for murder has doubled.

- am Ende (*end-position*)

  The number of youths arrested for murder has doubled <u>in 20 years</u>.

- im Satz (*mid-position*)

  Older people are <u>extremely</u> worried about the high crime rate.

Beachte:

- Wenn mehrere Adverbien in einem Satz stehen, ist die normale Reihenfolge: **Art und Weise – Ort – Zeit** (*manner – place – time*).

  The PM spoke <u>well</u> / <u>in the House of Commons</u> / <u>this morning</u>.

- Nach **Verben der Bewegung** steht die **Adverbiale des Ortes** unmittelbar **nach dem Verb**.

  He <u>drove</u> <u>to the station</u> in a taxi.

- Bei mehreren Zeitadverbien steht die **genauere Zeitangabe vor der allgemeineren**.

  He was born at <u>six o'clock</u> <u>on Christmas day</u> in <u>the year 1867</u>.

Vor dem Vollverb stehen gewöhnlich (d. h., wenn sie nicht besonders betont werden sollen):

- Adverbien der **unbestimmten Zeit** (*already, just, now, soon, still, then*)

  I have <u>already</u> <u>spoken</u> to the headmaster about our excursion.

- Adverbien der **unbestimmten Häufigkeit** (always, frequently, generally, hardly ever, never, occasionally, often, rarely, seldom, sometimes, usually)

When she was still at school Sandra <u>often worked</u> as a Saturday girl in Boots the Chemist.

Zur besonderen Betonung kann man Adverbien der unbestimmten Zeit oder Häufigkeit aber auch an den Anfang des Satzes stellen.

Sandra <u>usually</u> worked on Saturdays. (= normale Stellung)

<u>Sometimes</u> she helped on Fridays, too. (= betonte Stellung)

4 Übungen

1 Adjective or adverb – Choose the correct form.

Teenage drinking

In spite of the fact that in Britain you cannot buy alcohol _____ [1] if you are under 18, many youngsters drink _____ [2] before they have reached legal age. The case of 19-year-old Jane shows what harm alcohol can do. Drinking alcohol has played an important part in her life for a long time. She started drinking _____ [3] when she was 16. At that time she worked as a shop assistant. She tried very _____ [4] to conceal her dependency. At first, she drank only at home in her spare time, but _____ [5] she took bottles of spirits to work, hiding them _____ [6] in her locker. Her efficiency at work _____ [7] declined: she forgot what she was told to do, she was late for work, and she neglected her appearance.

When the manager told her that she had a drink problem, Jane denied it, but _____ [8] admitted that her drinking had got out of control and asked for help. Her employer helped her find a place in a special rehabilitation centre for young people, in east London.

Rehabilitation from dependency is a long-term process which requires patience and stamina. The path to

legal / legally
heavy / heavily

regular / regularly

hard / hardly

eventual / eventually

careful / carefully
gradual / gradually

final / finally

rehabilitation is not _____ ⁹. Although the centre is not a _____ ¹⁰ holiday home, the atmosphere seems _____ ¹¹ enough. The programme starts with a rather strict settling-in phase when residents can't go out alone and have to talk _____ ¹² about their problems and feelings in groups. Jane says: "When I came here I thought 'feelings groups' sounded stupid. But being here has built up my confidence _____ ¹³. And I don't feel that I'm the only alcoholic in the world."

To protect other residents, people who take to drinking again or behave _____ ¹⁴ are asked to leave. Although the regime in the centre does not suit everyone, staff and residents enjoy _____ ¹⁵ relationships. The team running the centre doesn't expect the young people to lead a life of _____ ¹⁶ abstinence in future, but they do hope that residents will understand why they developed a problem and return to a normal lifestyle. Jane's prospects look _____ ¹⁷ and her employer is prepared to give her a second chance.

easy/easily
comfortable/comfortably
happy/happily
open/openly
tremendous/tremendously
violent/violently
close/closely
total/totally
good/well

2 Adverb plus adjective – Choose a word from each box to form a combination of adverb and adjective. Complete the sentences. There is more than just one version possible.

absolutely – comparatively – seriously – completely – especially – fairly – fairly – unusually – generally – greatly – hardly – initially –widely

accepted – contributed – exaggerated – surprising – criticized – different – strict – dramatic – easy – injured – low – static – unfair

The truth about teenage crime

Many people tend to believe that life in general has become more dangerous and that juvenile crime in particular is on the increase. Sensationalist and often _widely exaggerated_ reports in the media have _____ ¹ to this view. It is _____ ² that TV news about violence and murders in big cities have contributed to the _____

_____[3] view that we are living in a world full of aggression. It cannot be denied that the _____[4] access to firearms plays a part in incidents of homicides among juveniles.

However, statistics paint a _____[5] picture and prove that complaints about violent teenagers are unjustified. There is no evidence of increasing violence or crime by urban or suburban youth. In fact, juvenile crime rates have fallen compared to three decades ago, with property offences and rape showing _____[6] de-creases. To some, the latest figures may seem _____[7] but they reflect reality. There are also fewer arrests of youths for curfew viola-tions, running away from home and truancy. However, the two offences show-ing the least decrease, robbery and assault, have remained _____ _____[8]. There are still too many cases of people becoming victims of gangs and being _____[9].

The overall decrease in crime is mainly due to the _____[10] application of police tactics and the introduction of youth curfews – an _____ _____[11] measure to keep youngsters off the streets at night-time. All in all, it would be _____[12] to blame teenagers for an increase in violence.

3   Complete the adjectives or adverbs in the following text.

Domestic violence

Domestic violence is not an insigni_____[1] problem. However, it is argu_____[2] the most under-reported and under-recorded crime. The number of women who become victims of domestic assaults is not known. It is estimated that only one in seven cases come to the attention of the police; thus its true extent remains unkn_____[3]. In the USA, a special hotline, the National Domestic Violence Hotline (NDVH), was established for women who were emoti_____[4] or physi_____[5] abused by their partners. Every month the confid_____[6] hotline receives more than 21,000 calls for help.

Until recent years, the police felt rather helpl_____[7] in their investigations of assault in the home. From the legal point of view it was difficult to arrest the assailant straight away. If the attacker was arrested, the victims, usu_____[8] wives or girlfriends, were afraid to give evidence. Conseq_____[9], the role of the police was larg_____[10] confined to talking to the parties and calming them down to prevent further violence. Only in extreme cases would the assailant be taken to court and the offence would mer_____¹¹ be recorded in the general category of assault.

In view of the drama_____¹² increasing number of incidents the police decided it was high time to work out a new strategy to tackle the problem. A committee, which comprised representatives of social services and women's groups, laid down the plans for a new scheme. Police policy quic_____¹³ changed from mediation in domestic disputes to one of intervention.

A number of speci_____¹⁴ domestic violence units were set up at police stations, where victims could give statements to speci_____¹⁵ trained officers in a comfor_____¹⁶ and sympathetic environment, rather than the usual sparsely and unwelcoming police station interview room. Each incident was recorded explic_____¹⁷ as a domestic assault and the figures were collected separ_____¹⁸. Not surpris_____¹⁹, the frequency of domestic violence soared immediately. The rise is statistic proof of the contin_____²⁰ success of a deliberate policy shift and more intensive police work.

It is also important to make the public aware of the crime because domestic violence also has a range of nega_____²¹ effects on children. They risk injury and even death by the abuser if they acciden_____²² get in the way of an attack or attempt to intervene to protect their mother.

4 Fill in suitable adjectives or adverbs from the boxes to complete the texts. You don't have to change the forms!

a) Young people and drugs

> especially – astonishing – largely – eventually – finally – recreational – initially – sole

In the past, most drugs were made from plants. That is to say, plants were grown and _____¹ converted into drugs such as coca paste, opium and marijuana. Over the years, these crude products were further processed to yield drugs like cocaine and heroin, and _____², in the 20th century, people found out how to make drugs from chemicals. These are called man-made, or synthetic, drugs and include speed, ecstasy, LSD, etc. These were _____³ manufactured for _____⁴ experimental reasons and only later were used for _____⁵

purposes. Now, however, with the increased size and scope of the drug trade, people set out to invent drugs _____⁶ for recreational human consumption.

Designer drug cocktails appear and disappear with _____ _____⁷ regularity. For the first time in human history, a whole industrial complex creates and produces drugs that are meant to be used outside and in defiance of social conventions for the _____⁸ purpose of "having fun."

b) **What's wrong with drug abuse?**

> regular – admirable – clear – free – negative – physiological – potentially – addictive – severely – unarguable – frequently – unpredictable

Substance abuse has many _____¹ physiological health effects, ranging from minor issues like digestion problems or respiratory infections, to _____² fatal diseases, like AIDS and hepatitis C. Of course, the effects depend on the drug and on the amount, the method and on how _____³ it is used. Some drugs are very _____⁴, like heroin, while others are less so. But the upshot is that _____⁵ drug abuse or sustained exposure to a drug – even for a short period of time – can cause _____⁶ dependence, which means that when the person stops taking drugs, he/she experiences physical withdrawal symptoms and a craving for the drug.

Drug abuse also causes brain damage. Again, depending on the drug, the strength and character of this damage varies. But one thing is _____ _____⁷, drug abuse affects the way the brain functions and alters its responses to the world. That is what psychoactive means, after all: something that acts on your brain. How _____⁸ drug abuse will affect your behaviour, actions, feelings and motivations is _____ _____⁹. By meddling in the natural ways the brain functions, abusers expose themselves to risks they may not even have imagined.

Finally, drug abuse damages the ability of people to act as free and conscious beings, capable of taking action to fulfil their needs. How _____ _____¹⁰ drug abusers are when they have no control over their actions or reactions is debatable. What is _____¹¹ is that by giving in to bio-chemical processes that are deviant, a drug abuser loses what makes humans _____¹² and unique.

5 Position of adverb (word order) – Join the following phrases to form a paragraph on Jury Service in Britain.

Jury Service

When someone is called to do Jury Service in Britain they are first of all sent an explanatory leaflet which explains what is going to happen and what they are supposed to do.

1   and / at a criminal trial / explains / this leaflet / what happens / your part in it

_____

_____

2   a member of the court staff / at court / more about the duties of jurors / on your first morning / will tell / you

_____

_____

3   for ten working days / jury service / lasts / normally

_____

_____

4   any difficulty / if a trial / if this would cause / is likely / to last longer, / you will be asked

_____

_____

Why have a Jury?

5   selected at random / than / there is no fairer way of deciding facts / to take twelve people

_____

_____

6   carefully / during the trial / is / their job / to all that takes place / to listen

_____

_____

7   a proper verdict / and pool their experience, common sense and wisdom / then / they go / to reach / to the juryroom

_____

_____

Jurors must be impartial

8 do not discuss / except other members of your jury / it is most important /
that / the case / with anybody / you

_____

_____

9 any discussion / in the privacy of the jury room / should take place /
when all the jurors are present

_____

_____

10 for any person / in any way / it is an offence / to influence / to try / you

_____

_____

11 about the case, / if anyone / immediately / or any police officer / speaks /
the matter / to the court / to you / you should report

_____

_____

Der Artikel • The Article

Der korrekte Gebrauch des bestimmten *(the)* bzw. unbestimmten *(a/an)* Artikels im Englischen gehört zu den schwierigsten Kapiteln der Grammatik. Die richtige Verwendung hängt nämlich von mehreren Faktoren ab, z. B. von der Art des Substantivs oder vom Kontext. Doch glücklicherweise hat eine fehlerhafte Verwendung keine negativen Konsequenzen für die praktische Kommunikation. Daher ist es sinnvoll, sich nur die Fälle einzuprägen, in denen sich die Verwendung des Artikels im Englischen vom Gebrauch im Deutschen besonders deutlich unterscheidet.

1 Bestimmter Artikel • Definite Article

Ohne bestimmten Artikel stehen:

- **abstrakte Begriffe** (z. B. *agriculture, life, nature*)

  Life is hard.

- Bezeichnungen für **Institutionen** (wenn nicht das konkrete Gebäude gemeint ist, in dem die betreffende Institution untergebracht ist)

  British boarding schools are being heavily criticized.
  Few people go to church these days.

- **Ortsbezeichnungen**

  Oxford Street, Charing Cross Road

- **Ländernamen**

  Switzerland, Turkey, Norway

- **Eigennamen von Bergen**

  Ben Nevis, Mont Blanc, Mount Everest

- **Eigennamen von Seen**

  Lake Geneva, Lake Windermere

Beachte besonders: Der Superlativ *most* hat vor Substantiven ohne bestimmten Artikel die Bedeutung ‚die meisten, der Großteil‘.

Most pupils don't like getting up early in the morning.

Mit bestimmtem Artikel stehen:

- **abstrakte Begriffe**, die **näher bestimmt** oder **eingegrenzt** werden

  We don't know very much about the life of William Shakespeare.

- **Gebäudebezeichnungen** (wenn vom Gebäude selbst, nicht aber von der Institution die Rede ist)

  He remembers standing at the entrance of the school.
  The church Bill goes to is called St. Mary's.

- **Eigennamen im Plural**

  the Taylors, the Walker Brothers

- **einige Länder**

  the Falklands, the USA, the UK

- **Eigennamen von Flüssen** und **Meeren**

  the Thames, the Atlantic, the Baltic

- der Superlativ *most* in Ausdrücken wie to *make the most of* ('das Beste machen aus'), *for the most part* ('zum größten Teil')

  Although you might hate school now and then, you must try and make the most of it.

Beachte: Steht der bestimmte Artikel **vor beiden Attributen**, dann steht das folgende Substantiv im Singular.

In the 16th and the 17th century acting was not a socially accepted activity.
Im 16. und 17. Jahrhundert war die Schauspielerei keine gesellschaftlich anerkannte Tätigkeit.

Aber: Steht der bestimmte Artikel nur **vor einem der Attribute**, dann steht das folgende Substantiv im Plural.

In the 16th and 17th centuries acting was not a socially accepted activity.

2 Unbestimmter Artikel • Indefinite Article

Ohne unbestimmten Artikel stehen **Funktions-, Titel- und Rangbezeichnungen**.

Barack Obama was elected President (of the USA) in 2008.
Harry Beason held the rank of Captain of the Royal Navy.

Der **unbestimmte Artikel** wird benutzt, um die Nationalität oder die Zugehörigkeit zu einem Beruf zu bezeichnen.
Im Deutschen verwenden wir in beiden Fällen **keinen** Artikel.

Mr Pertwee is a businessman and lives in Colchester.
Mr Pertwee ist Geschäftsmann und lebt in Colchester.

Gregory's father is a Scot.
Gregorys Vater ist Schotte.

3   Übungen

6   Definite or indefinite article – Decide whether to use definite article *the*, indefinite article *a/an* or no article at all.

Have you ever thought of emigrating?

According to _____[1] recent survey _____[2] number of British people opting to move abroad has seen _____[3] significant rise. Potential emigrants are concerned about _____[4] economic situation and _____[5] state of affairs in the country. Consequently quite _____[6] few would like to emigrate and start _____[7] new life abroad. But this has become very difficult today, indeed.

_____[8] traditional countries British people used to emigrate to are: Canada, Australia, _____[9] United States and New Zealand. But none of these countries accepts all of _____[10] applicants who would like to come. Only those who have completed their apprenticeships really have a chance. The countries are looking for _____[11] skilled emigrants, e.g. people who have enough qualifications to find _____[12] job, thus adding to _____[13] prosperity of the economy and not to _____[14] dole queues of their new homelands.

Anybody willing to emigrate ought to think twice about this decisive move. If you leave, you must be prepared to build up your life in _____[15] completely new and different surroundings. This is _____[16] great opportunity, but also an enormous challenge to _____[17] people's ability to adapt.

By the way, there seem to be some good possibilities for _____[18] sheep farming in _____[19] Falklands, but _____[20] most people wouldn't like to go there.

7 Definite or indefinite article – Put in *a/an* or *the* where necessary.

Job search skills for young people

What will you do after _____¹ school? Go to _____² university or enter _____³ business life? If you think of applying for a job – be it as _____⁴ secretary or as _____⁵ managing director – you will almost certainly have to go for an interview. Today, _____⁶ most employers attach great importance to a personal conversation which is usually carried out by the personnel manager of the firm and which will be about your former activities, your educational background, language qualifications, etc. In addition, details of your contract, pay and conditions of work will be discussed. The experts at the Jobcentre are concerned about your safety as _____⁷ jobseeker, therefore they provide _____⁸ leaflet with some good advice. This is what it says:

Be alert – be safe when jobseeking

The vast majority of _____⁹ job interviews are perfectly straightforward. You attend _____¹⁰ interview and everything goes well. But whether you hear about _____¹¹ opportunity through your Jobcentre or through _____¹² advertisement in _____¹³ newspaper, there are _____¹⁴ few common sense rules that you should always remember:

Do
- tell _____¹⁵ friend or relative where you are going and what time you expect to be back,
- arrange to be collected from the interview if it takes place outside _____¹⁶ working hours,
- find out as much as you can about the company before the interview, especially if there are no details in _____¹⁷ job advert,
- make sure that _____¹⁸ interview takes place at _____¹⁹ employer's premises or, if not, in _____²⁰ public place.

Don't
- apply for _____²¹ job which seems to offer too much money for very little work,
- agree to continue the interview over _____²² drinks or _____²³ meal, even if it seems to be going very well,
- let the interviewer steer _____²⁴ conversation towards _____²⁵ personal subjects that have nothing to do with the job,
- accept _____²⁶ lift home from the interviewer.

Jobcentres make every effort to ensure that the vacancies they display are genuine and that _____²⁷ safety of jobseekers is never put at _____²⁸ risk. They also investigate every complaint about an employer using the Jobcentre's services, so if you do run into _____²⁹ difficulties, you should let them know straight away.

8 Definite or indefinite article – Put in *a/an* or *the* where necessary.

Interviews

It is natural to feel nervous about _____¹ prospect of _____² interview but _____³ employer obviously thinks you are suitable otherwise they would not be interviewing you! If you feel confident about yourself and your capabilities this will come across in _____⁴ interview.

An interview is _____⁵ two way process – it gives _____⁶ employer _____⁷ chance to find out more about you and how you match up to your application plus it gives you a chance to find out if _____⁸ job and the employer live up to your expectations.

It is important to prepare for _____⁹ interview, not just turn up! This will make you confident and shows _____¹⁰ interviewer that you are motivated and serious about wanting to work for them.

There is _____¹¹ wide range of resources available on applying for jobs. You will find useful material in books, video or CD collections or online.

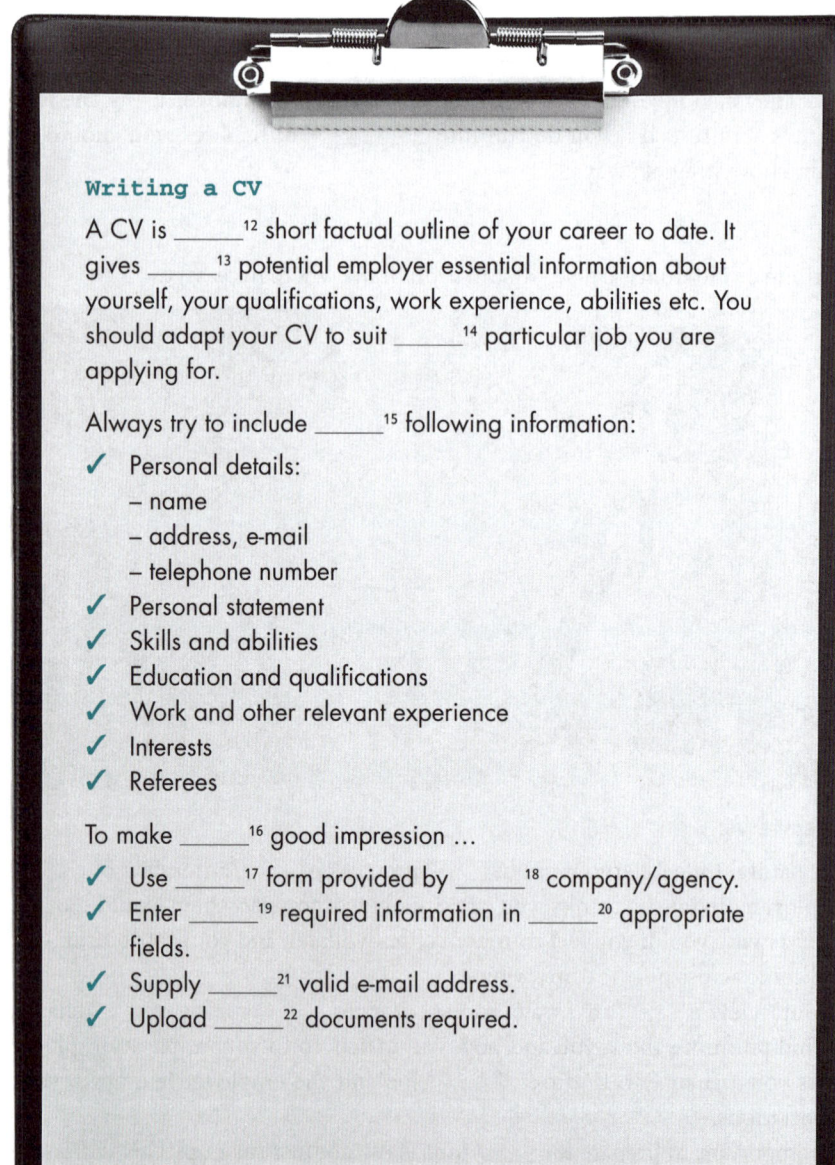

Writing a CV

A CV is _____[12] short factual outline of your career to date. It gives _____[13] potential employer essential information about yourself, your qualifications, work experience, abilities etc. You should adapt your CV to suit _____[14] particular job you are applying for.

Always try to include _____[15] following information:

✔ Personal details:
  – name
  – address, e-mail
  – telephone number
✔ Personal statement
✔ Skills and abilities
✔ Education and qualifications
✔ Work and other relevant experience
✔ Interests
✔ Referees

To make _____[16] good impression …

✔ Use _____[17] form provided by _____[18] company/agency.
✔ Enter _____[19] required information in _____[20] appropriate fields.
✔ Supply _____[21] valid e-mail address.
✔ Upload _____[22] documents required.

Bedingungssätze •
Conditional Sentences

1   Form und Bildung

Ein vollständiger Bedingungssatz besteht aus zwei Satzteilen: dem konditionalen Nebensatz (*if-clause*) und dem Hauptsatz (*main clause*). Der Nebensatz nennt die Bedingung,
unter der das im Hauptsatz genannte Geschehen eintritt. Im Hauptsatz wird je nach Art
der genannten Bedingung [siehe S. 18] *conditional* oder *conditional perfect* verwendet.
So werden die Formen gebildet:

1.1   Konditional I • Conditional

could / would + Infinitiv	We <u>would</u> <u>reduce</u> the amount of waste if we used less disposable bottles. *Wir <u>würden</u> die Abfallmenge <u>verringern</u>, wenn wir weniger Einwegflaschen benutzen würden.*

1.2   Konditional II • Conditional Perfect

could / would + *have* + *past participle*	We <u>would</u> <u>have</u> <u>reduced</u> the amount of waste if we had used more return bottles. *Wir <u>hätten</u> die Abfallmenge <u>verringert</u>, wenn wir mehr Mehrwegflaschen benutzt hätten.*

2   Gebrauch

Die Bedingungen, die im konditionalen Nebensatz (*if-clause*) genannt werden, teilt man
in zwei Gruppen ein: objektiv **erfüllbare** und **nicht erfüllbare** Bedingungen. Die nicht
erfüllbaren Bedingungen werden wiederum in zwei Untergruppen (unwahrscheinliche
und unmögliche Bedingungen) eingeteilt, sodass man insgesamt **drei Typen von Bedingungen** (und damit auch drei Typen von *if*-Sätzen) unterscheidet.

Typ 1: Erfüllbare Bedingung

Der Sprecher hält die Bedingung für erfüllbar.

if-Satz	Hauptsatz
If we <u>eat</u> less meat,	we'll <u>limit</u> global warming.
Wenn wir weniger Fleisch essen,	*werden wir die globale Erwärmung eindämmen.*

Typ 2: Nicht erfüllbare (unwahrscheinliche) Bedingung

Der Sprecher hält es für unwahrscheinlich, dass die Bedingung erfüllt wird.

if-Satz	Hauptsatz
If we all <u>became</u> vegetarians today,	we <u>would stop</u> climate change.
Wenn wir alle heute Vegetarier würden,	*würden wir den Klimawandel stoppen.*

Typ 3: Nicht mehr erfüllbare (unmögliche) Bedingung

Die Bedingung kann nicht mehr erfüllt werden, da sie sich auf die Vergangenheit bezieht.

if-Satz	Hauptsatz
If we <u>had reduced</u> global meat production already,	we <u>would have saved</u> huge amounts of carbon dioxide.
Wenn wir die globale Fleischproduktion schon reduziert hätten,	*hätten wir riesige Mengen an Kohlendioxid gespart.*

Die Zeit im Hauptsatz ist abhängig von der Art der Bedingung, die im *if*-Satz erscheint. Man spricht hier von der Zeitenfolge *(sequence of tenses)* [siehe auch S. 19].

Das deutsche **‚wenn'** kann **zwei** verschiedene **Bedeutungen** haben:

- temporal
  ‚wenn/sobald' = *when*

  <u>When</u> the soil cannot absorb the heavy rains, floods occur.

  Wenn (= <u>Sobald</u>) der Boden die starken Niederschläge nicht aufnehmen kann, kommt es zu Überschwemmungen.

- konditional
  ‚wenn/falls' = *if*

  <u>If</u> factory farms do not stop clearing forests to create pastureland, soil erosion will increase.

  Wenn (= <u>Falls</u>) industrielle Viehzuchtbetriebe nicht aufhören, Wälder abzuholzen, um Weideland zu schaffen, wird die Bodenerosion zunehmen.

3 Vertiefung

3.1 Zeitenfolge • The Sequence of Tenses

Typ 1: Erfüllbare Bedingung *(Probable / Open Condition)*

Im *if*-Satz steht eine Bedingung, die erfüllt werden kann.

> Wenn im *if*-Satz *present tense* verwendet wird, steht im **Hauptsatz *will-future***.

if-Satz	Hauptsatz
If we <u>reduce</u> the number of cars on the roads,	we'<u>ll stop</u> the dying of our forests.
Wenn wir die Zahl der Autos auf den Straßen verringern,	*werden wir das Waldsterben beenden.*

> Bei diesen erfüllbaren Bedingungen (Typ 1) kann im **Hauptsatz** auch das **Präsens** stehen. Der Sprecher möchte dann ausdrücken, dass **unter** den **gleichen Bedingungen** immer wieder das **gleiche Ergebnis** eintritt (allgemeingültige Aussage).

if-Satz	Hauptsatz
If we <u>cut</u> down more rain forests,	the earth's climate <u>is</u> affected.
Wenn wir mehr Regenwälder abholzen,	*wird das Weltklima beeinträchtigt.*

Typ 2: Unwahrscheinliche Bedingung *(Improbable Condition)*

Im *if*-Satz steht eine Bedingung, deren Erfüllung der Sprecher für eher unwahrscheinlich hält.

> Wenn im *if*-Satz *past tense* verwendet wird, steht im **Hauptsatz *conditional***.
> Typ 1 und Typ 2 **unterscheiden sich nicht zeitlich** voneinander! Die Vergangenheitsform in Typ 2 ist der so genannte modale Konjunktiv, mit dem der Sprecher ausdrücken möchte, dass er die Erfüllung der Bedingung für unwahrscheinlich hält. Theoretisch wäre es zwar möglich, die Bedingung zu erfüllen, aber der Sprecher glaubt nicht daran. Dieser Typ 2 birgt eine häufige Fehlerquelle für den deutschen Lerner, wenn er vom Deutschen her übersetzt. Hier darf *would* **nicht im *if*-Satz** stehen.

if-Satz	Hauptsatz
If all countries <u>agreed</u> on a strategy to reduce emissions,	we <u>would succeed</u> in fighting climate change.
Wenn alle Länder sich auf eine Strategie zur Reduzierung von Emissionen einigen würden,	*hätten wir Erfolg im Kampf gegen den Klimawandel.*

Typ 3: Unmögliche Bedingung *(Impossible Condition)*

Im *if*-Satz steht eine Bedingung, die nicht mehr erfüllt werden kann, da sie sich auf die Vergangenheit bezieht. Somit stellt diese „Bedingung" eine bloße Annahme dar.

> Wenn im *if-Satz past perfect* verwendet wird, steht im **Hauptsatz** *conditional perfect*.

if-Satz	Hauptsatz
If the Brazilian government <u>had prohibited</u> the cutting down of the rain forests earlier,	less soil <u>would have turned</u> into desert.
Wenn die brasilianische Regierung das Abholzen der Regenwälder früher verboten hätte,	*wäre weniger Boden zu Wüste geworden.*

3.2 Sonderfälle

would im *if*-Satz

> Normalerweise werden *would* und *should* im *if*-Satz nicht verwendet. Es gibt jedoch **zwei Ausnahmen:**

- wenn man etwas für **besonders unwahrscheinlich** hält *(unlikely action)*

  <u>If</u> oil slicks <u>should spread</u> into the bay, birds and fish would be killed.
  Wenn der Ölteppich doch in die Bucht eindringen sollte, würden Vögel und Fische ums Leben kommen.

- wenn man eine **besonders höfliche Aufforderung** oder **Bitte** formulieren möchte *(polite request)*.

  <u>If</u> you <u>would</u> kindly <u>deposit</u> the packaging over here, we'll dispose of it properly.
  Wenn Sie die Verpackungen bitte hier ablegen würden, werden wir sie entsprechend entsorgen.

unless im *if*-Satz

> Statt *if not* kann im *if*-Satz *unless* verwendet werden (ebenso: *in case* statt *if*).

if-Satz	Hauptsatz
<u>Unless</u> the oil spill is cleared up immediately,	more seabirds will die.
Wenn der Ölteppich nicht sofort beseitigt wird,	*werden noch mehr Seevögel sterben.*

was / were im *if*-Satz

were wird immer verwendet bei der Formulierung *If I were you ...* (*,Wenn ich an deiner Stelle wäre ...' / ,An deiner Stelle ...'*).

if-Satz	Hauptsatz
If I were you,	I would leave all wrappings in the shop.
Ich an deiner Stelle	*würde ich die ganzen Umverpackungen im Laden lassen.*

Die richtige Form lautet zwar **were**, diese wird jedoch insbesondere **umgangssprachlich** immer häufiger durch **was** ersetzt.

if-Satz	Hauptsatz
If it wasn't so inconvenient,	many shoppers would leave the wrappings in the shops.
Wenn es nicht so unpraktisch wäre,	*würden viele Käufer die Umverpackungen im Laden lassen.*

Kommasetzung

Der *if*-Satz wird vom Hauptsatz nur dann durch ein Komma abgetrennt, wenn er am Anfang steht.

if-Satz	Hauptsatz
If meat and dairy were produced in environmentally friendly ways,	we would save resources.

Aber:

We would save resources_	if meat and dairy were produced in environmentally friendly ways.

4 Übungen

9 If-clauses – Fill in the right form of the verbs in brackets. Future tense should be used in the main clauses.

A safer environment

We ___*will be able to reduce*___ (can, reduce) pollution considerably if people use more renewable energy sources.

If we want to protect our environment, rich and poor countries _____ _____[1] (must/cooperate) more closely.

We'll have to take stronger measures if we _____[2] (be to/stop) global warming.

We _____[3] (can/save) our ozone shield unless we reduce emissions of greenhouse gases.

Unless we can stop population growth, the biggest global environmental problem

_____[4]

(solve).

If we wish to reduce emission of greenhouse gases world-wide, we _____

_____[5] (must/consider) reducing our meat consumption.

Unless economics and environmentalism go hand in hand, saving our environment _____[6] (be) a successful enterprise.

If people are to accept wind farms, advocates of renewable energy _____ _____[7] (must/convince) the general public that wind powered electricity is cheaper than power generated from a traditional coal plant.

Unless we manage to recycle more rubbish, we _____[8] (can/conserve) raw materials.

If we can persuade more people to sort their domestic waste, waste disposal _____[9] (be) easier.

If we tell children from an early age how important it is to protect our environment, they _____[10] (be) better consumers later.

10 If-clauses – Fill in the right form of the verb in brackets. Past tense should be used in the if-clause.

Caring for the environment

Many nuclear plants _could be shut down_ (can, shut down) if more nations decided to promote alternative power sources.

If less washing-up liquid was used in households, the sewage plants _____ _____[1] (can/cope) with the waste water more easily.

If farmers used less fertilizers, our ground water _____[2] (be) less loaded with nitrates.

If people _____[3] (must/pay) for the collection of their household rubbish according to weight, they would be given more incentive to reduce their waste.

If the public _____[4] (be) prepared to pay a bit more for "green" washing-powder, the industry could better market it.

There would be fewer cars on the roads if employees who work in the same factories _____[5] (drive) to work together.

If bus connections _____[6] (be) better, especially in the country, more people would use public transport.

If we stopped using the seas as cheap dumping grounds for toxic waste, marine life _____[7] (may/save).

If companies _____[8] (receive) more incentive from the state, they would be more enthusiastic about developing "green" products.

Managers argue that if the government passed even stricter laws concerning production methods, they _____ _____[9] (be) tempted to transfer production to foreign countries where regulations are less strict.

11 If-clauses – Rewrite these sentences using an if-construction.

Keep our planet clean

0 Wind turbines are still very noisy. That's (one reason) why people protest vehemently against wind farms in their neighbourhood.
If wind turbines were less noisy, people would not protest so vehemently ...

1 Many packages are not environment-friendly; that's why it is difficult and expensive to dispose of them properly.

2 Many wrappings are needed due to hygiene requirements; that's why we have to keep them.

3 Some people are still used to throwing everything into one bin; that's why it is impossible to burn all the rubbish.

4 Not all people sort their household waste; that's why it must be done in special recycling plants.

5 Plastic containers are still too cheap; that's why they are used a lot.

6 Many people are too lazy to take their empty bottles to the bottle bank; that's why their dustbins are so full.

7 Many smokers aren't environmentally conscious; that's why they throw their cigarette ends all over the place.

8 Yellow sacks are distributed free of charge; that's why irresponsible people use them instead of dustbins.

12 If-clauses – Rewrite these sentences using an if-construction.

Oil tanker disaster

In October 2011, a container ship ran aground on a reef near Tauranga in New Zealand. The ship, called the MV Rena, was loaded with more than 1,300 containers, some of which went overboard, and 1,900 tonnes of oil, which spilled into the sea, killing more than one thousand animals.

0   The ship ran aground on a reef; that's why it listed badly.

If the ship hadn't run aground on a reef, it wouldn't have listed badly.

1   The ship's hull was cracked; that's why some of the oil leaked.

_____

2   The ship was very close to the shore; that's why so many animals were killed by spilled oil.

_____

3   The oil reached popular surfing spots; that's why MARITIME NEW ZEALAND had to close some of the beaches along the coast to the public.

_____

4   Thousands of volunteers helped to clean the beaches; that's why many seabirds survived.

_____

5   There were strong winds; that's why some containers were washed overboard.

_____

6   Some of the containers carried hazardous material; that's why the authorities worried that contact with water could lead to dangerous chemical reactions.

_____

7   The weather conditions off the coast were very rough; that's why the salvage team had to wait with their rescue operation.

_____

8   The weather calmed down at last; that's why the salvage experts could pump the remaining oil to a barge.

_____

Annotations
to list badly = *schwere Schlagseite haben* / hull = *Rumpf* / salvage = *Bergung*

13

City of London

Fire safety advice for residents

Please read the following advice from the City of London's Fire Officer on what you should do in the event of a fire and of precautions you should take to prevent fires occurring.

You must ensure that you are familiar with your means of escape (details are given in the residential handbook) and that you do not impede access to these escape routes.

Do not wait until a fire occurs – read this guide and decide the best way for you and your family to get out of your home or out of the building if there is a fire elsewhere. There may be more than one way out. If you and all other people in the building observe the following rules, you will be much safer and less likely to start a fire or be injured in one.

Fire advice:

- Make sure that smoke alarms (if fitted) in your home are working. If not fitted, consider installing them to give vital early warning of fire.
- Do not store anything in your hall or corridor, especially things that will burn easily.
- Use the fixed heating system in your home. If this is not possible, use only a convector heater in your hall or corridor. Do not use any form of radiant heater, especially one with either a flame (calor gas or paraffin) or a radiant element (electric bar fire).
- Leave the affected room immediately together with anybody else. Close the door behind you.
- Do not stay behind and try to put the fire out.
- Tell everybody else in your home about the fire and get everyone to leave. Close your front door and leave the building.
- Only use the balcony if it is part of the escape route and you are not able to use your normal exit route.

If you see or hear a fire in another part of the building:

- It will often be safe for you to stay in your home.
- Call the Fire Brigade.
- Close all doors and windows. If smoke or heat affects your flat, leave at once.
- If necessary, the Fire Brigade will advise you to leave your home. Evacuation of buildings should only be undertaken by the Fire Brigade.

http://www.cityoflondon.gov.uk/Corporation/LGNL_Services/Housing/Private_housing/fire_safety.htm

Read the leaflet about how to avoid fires at home and what to do in an emergency. Make sentences using if-constructions (preferably second condition).

Fire safety – What would you do?

0   no fire alarm fitted in home

   If I didn't have a fire alarm fitted in my home, I would install one.

1   no separate room for storing things

2   no fixed heating system

3   fire breaks out in your room

4   there are other people in the house

5   normal escape routes blocked

6   fire breaks out in another part of the building

7   smoke comes into your flat

8   evacuate the building?

Das Gerundium · The Gerund

1 Form und Bildung

Als „Gerundium" *(gerund)* bezeichnet man ein Verb, das als Substantiv verwendet wird. Im Englischen wie im Deutschen wird dieses „Verbalsubstantiv" vom Infinitiv abgeleitet.

Infinitiv + *-ing*	My aunt Nancy has always been interested in <u>reading</u> books.

2 Gebrauch

2.1 Funktionen des Gerundiums im Satz

1. Das Gerundium als **Subjekt** eines Satzes.
   Es steht z. B. nach:

   Reading books is fun.

   - *there is no*
     (‚es lässt sich nicht')

     There is no <u>denying</u> that films are more popular than books.
     Es lässt sich nicht leugnen, dass Filme beliebter sind als Bücher.

   - *it's no use/no good*
     (‚es hat keinen Zweck')

     It's no use <u>doing</u> your homework with the radio on full blast.
     Es hat keinen Zweck, seine Hausaufgaben <u>zu machen</u>, wenn das Radio in voller Lautstärke läuft.

   - *it's (not) worthwhile*
     (‚es lohnt sich [nicht]')

     It's worthwhile <u>studying</u> the old poets.
     Es lohnt sich, die alten Dichter <u>zu lesen</u>.

2. Das Gerundium als **Teil des Prädikats** *(predicative complement)*, z. B. nach *busy, near, like, worth*.

   James was <u>busy</u> <u>trying</u> out the latest software.
   James war damit <u>beschäftigt</u>, das neueste Computerprogramm <u>auszuprobieren</u>.

3. Das Gerundium als **Objekt**
   [siehe Liste der Verben S. 31].

   Anyone who doesn't know his subject, <u>dreads</u> <u>answering</u> examination questions.
   Wer nichts von seinem Fach versteht, <u>fürchtet sich</u> davor, Prüfungsaufgaben <u>zu beantworten</u>.

2.2 Gerundium nach Präpositionen

Adjektiv + Präposition + Gerundium

to be afraid of = *Angst haben vor*
to be ashamed of = *sich schämen für*
to be clever at = *geschickt sein in*
to be crazy about = *verrückt sein nach*
to be disappointed about = *enttäuscht sein über*
to be famous for = *berühmt sein für*
to be fond of = *begeistert sein von*
to be good/bad at = *etwas gut/schlecht können*
to be interested in = *interessiert sein an*
to be keen on = *etwas gerne tun*
to be proud of = *stolz sein auf*
to be sick of = *genug haben von*
to be sorry for = *leid tun, dass*
to be worried about = *sich Sorgen machen um*

Sam was <u>good at</u> <u>writing</u> essays, so quite a few classmates asked him for his help.
Sam konnte gut Aufsätze schreiben, weshalb ihn viele Klassenkameraden um Hilfe baten.

Nomen + Präposition + Gerundium

chance of = *Chance, Aussicht (zu)*
danger of = *Gefahr (zu)*
difficulty in = *Schwierigkeit (zu)*
hopes of = *Hoffnung (auf/zu)*
idea of = *Vorstellung (zu)*
possibility of = *Möglichkeit (zu)*
reason for = *Grund für*
way of = *Art und Weise (zu)*

Chloe was in <u>danger of</u> <u>failing</u> the exam for the second time.
Chloe lief Gefahr, die Prüfung zum zweiten Mal nicht zu bestehen.

Verb + Präposition + Gerundium

to agree with = *einverstanden sein mit*
to apologize for = *sich entschuldigen für*
to believe in = *glauben an*
to complain about = *sich beklagen über*
to consist of = *bestehen aus*
to dream of = *träumen von*
to insist on = *auf etwas bestehen*

to look forward to = *sich freuen auf*
to rely on = *sich verlassen auf*
to succeed in = *es schaffen (zu)*
to talk of/about = *reden von / sprechen über*
to worry about = *sich Sorgen machen um*

Paul <u>succeeded in</u> <u>passing</u> the test without any difficulties.
Paul schaffte es, die Prüfung ohne Schwierigkeiten zu bestehen.

3 Vertiefung

3.1 Gerundium in Verbindung mit bestimmten Verben

to admit = *zugeben*
to anticipate = *vorwegnehmen, voraussehen*
to avoid = *vermeiden*
to consider = *erwägen*
to defer = *verschieben*
to delay = *verschieben, verzögern*
to deny = *leugnen*
to detest = *verabscheuen*
to dread = *fürchten*
to enjoy = *genießen*
to excuse = *entschuldigen*
to fancy = *Gefallen finden an*
to finish = *beenden*
to forgive = *verzeihen*
to imagine = *sich vorstellen*
to involve = *umfassen, mit sich bringen*
to keep = *fortfahren, weitermachen*
to mind = *etwas haben gegen*
to miss = *vermissen*
to pardon = *verzeihen*
to postpone = *verschieben*
to prevent = *(ver-)hindern*
to recollect = *sich erinnern an*
to resent = *übelnehmen*
to resist = *widerstehen*
to risk = *wagen*
to save = *retten, bewahren*
to stop = *aufhören*
to suggest = *vorschlagen*
to understand = *verstehen*

Poor Jenny had a terrible cold; she couldn't <u>avoid</u> <u>sneezing</u> throughout the play.

I cannot <u>imagine</u> <u>being</u> an actor.

The girls in the class <u>suggested</u> <u>reading</u> "Romeo and Juliet".

3.2 Gerundium und Infinitiv mit unterschiedlicher Bedeutung

Einige Verben ändern ihre Bedeutung, je nachdem, ob nach ihnen das Gerundium oder der Infinitiv steht.

to forget

Gerundium	Infinitiv
I shall not <u>forget</u> <u>reading</u> Shakespeare's "Macbeth" for the first time.	I shall not <u>forget</u> <u>to read</u> Shakespeare's "Macbeth".
Ich werde nicht vergessen, wie ich zum ersten Mal Shakespeares „Macbeth" las.	*Ich werde nicht vergessen, Shakespeares „Macbeth" zu lesen.*
[= in der Vergangenheit, früher einmal]	[= in Zukunft]

to like, to hate, to prefer

Gerundium	Infinitiv
I <u>like</u>/<u>hate</u> <u>going</u> to the theatre.	I <u>like</u>/<u>hate</u> <u>to go</u> to the theatre tonight.
Ich gehe (überhaupt nicht) gerne ins Theater.	*Ich möchte heute Abend (nicht) ins Theater gehen.*
[= im Allgemeinen, regelmäßig]	[= einmal, Einzelfall]

to regret

Gerundium	Infinitiv
I <u>regret</u> <u>missing</u> (= having missed) the play on TV.	I <u>regret</u> <u>to miss</u> the play on TV.
Es tut mir leid, dass ich das Stück im Fernsehen verpasst habe.	*Es tut mir leid, dass ich das Stück im Fernsehen nicht sehen kann. (= verpassen muss)*
[= früher]	[= jetzt]

to remember

Gerundium	Infinitiv
I <u>remember</u> <u>reading</u> the final scene of the play.	I must <u>remember</u> <u>to read</u> the final scene of the play.
Ich erinnere mich, dass ich die Schlussszene des Stücks las.	*Ich muss daran denken, die Schlussszene des Stücks zu lesen.*
[= in der Vergangenheit]	[= in Zukunft]

to stop

Gerundium	Infinitiv
I stopped reading the scene in which Banquo's ghost appears.	I stopped to read the scene in which Banquo's ghost appears.
Ich hörte damit auf, die Szene zu lesen, in der Banquos Geist auftritt.	*Ich hielt inne (d. h. hörte mit etwas auf), um die Szene zu lesen, in der Banquos Geist auftritt.*
[= ‚mit etwas aufhören‘, ‚etwas aufgeben‘]	[= ‚mit etwas aufhören, um etwas anderes zu tun‘]

to try

Gerundium	Infinitiv
I shan't try getting any tickets for the first performance of "Macbeth" at Stratford this year – it's no use anyway.	I've tried to get tickets for the first performance of "Macbeth" at Stratford this year – but in vain.
Ich werde dieses Jahr gar nicht erst versuchen, Karten für die Premiere von „Macbeth" in Stratford zu bekommen – es hat sowieso keinen Zweck.	*Ich habe versucht, Karten für die Premiere von „Macbeth" in Stratford zu bekommen – aber vergeblich.*
[= ‚einen Test machen‘, ‚etwas ausprobieren‘]	[= ‚eine ernsthafte Anstrengung unternehmen‘, ‚sich anstrengen‘]

3.3 Gerundium mit eigenem Subjekt

Das **Subjekt** des Satzes und das Subjekt des Gerundiums sind **identisch**.	Zoe doesn't like reading in bed at night. *Zoe (selbst) liest abends im Bett nicht gerne.* [= ein Subjekt]
Aber: Wenn das **Subjekt des Gerundiums** nicht auch **Subjekt des Satzes** ist, muss es **gesondert genannt** werden.	Zoe doesn't like Tom reading in bed at night. *Zoe mag es nicht, dass/wenn Tom abends im Bett noch liest.* [= zwei verschiedene Subjekte]
• Das **zweite Subjekt** steht **vor dem Gerundium**.	Zoe doesn't like Tom eating in bed either.
• Es kann aber auch als **Personalpronomen** oder **Possessivpronomen** wiedergegeben werden.	Zoe doesn't like him/his eating in bed either. *Zoe mag es auch nicht, dass/wenn er abends im Bett noch isst.*

3.4 Gerundium anstelle eines Adverbialsatzes

Ähnlich wie bei der Partizipialkonstruktion kann man mit dem Gerundium einen **Adverbialsatz der Zeit verkürzen.**

Adverbialsatz	Gerundiumkonstruktion
<u>When</u> Sue <u>arrived</u> at the classroom, she realized that she had forgotten to do her French homework.	<u>On arriving</u> at the classroom Sue realized that she had forgotten to do her French homework.

Als Sue am Klassenzimmer ankam, merkte sie, dass sie vergessen hatte, ihre Französischhausaufgaben zu machen.

Auf die gleiche Weise kann man auch einen **Adverbialsatz des Grundes verkürzen.**

Adverbialsatz	Gerundiumkonstruktion
<u>As he learnt</u> his French words better than usual Jack managed to improve his marks.	<u>By learning</u> his French words better than usual Jack managed to improve his marks.

Weil Jack seine Französischvokabeln besser als sonst lernte, konnte er seine Noten verbessern.

4 Übungen

14 Gerund as predicative complement – Rewrite these sentences replacing the underlined words by one of these expressions. Some phrases might fit more than once.

> cannot stop – possibility of – there is no – there's no way of – to be sick of – how about – to succeed in – to be tired of – to be worthwhile – to dream of – to enjoy – to give up – to have difficulty in – to look forward to – to be interested in

To write or to act, that's (not really) the question

All students in my class <u>don't like it when they have to write</u> essays on William Shakespeare.

All students in my class are sick of writing essays on William Shakespeare.

I think everybody agrees that it's <u>quite a good idea to read</u>[1] Shakespeare at school.

_____

Our teacher treats Shakespeare as "sacred" – he just can't <u>give up that habit</u>[2].

_____

We spent ages on Shakespeare's "The Tempest" – and we <u>hated that</u>[3].

_____

We <u>didn't like it when we had to go</u>⁴ through a text passage again and again!

Our teacher thought that <u>it would not be too difficult for us to write</u>⁵ a test paper on the play.

I think, most students would <u>like to perform</u>⁶ one of Shakespeare's plays very much.

That's why my friend Martin and I formed a drama group of our own; <u>our hobby is to act</u>⁷.

But <u>it was difficult for us to choose</u>⁸ a play which we could perform.

Some members of our group would have liked to produce "A Midsummer Night's Dream", but many roles were quite difficult and there were so many players needed – <u>we'd never be able to perform that play, we couldn't dream of it</u>⁹.

We didn't really know which play to choose because we wanted to avoid the possibility <u>that members of our group might feel</u>¹⁰ that they were not needed.

One night, Martin suggested, "<u>Couldn't we stage</u>¹¹ a play with just a few characters in it?"

Last week we <u>managed to pick</u>¹² a play that was suitable for us: John Priestley's "An Inspector Calls".

We're <u>glad that we're going to spend</u>¹³ the following weeks on this play.

Although most of us think that we have chosen the right play after all, some still worry [14] about where to get all the costumes and props which are necessary for the play.

_____

_____

It's absolutely impossible to tell [15] in advance whether we will succeed or not – and that's what's exciting about it.

_____

_____

You cannot deny that [16] students have more fun when they act in a play rather than when they just sit in the classroom and listen to a teacher reciting Shakespeare.

_____

_____

It would really be great if we tried [17] to produce more plays at school.

_____

15   Gerund after prepositions – Use the verbs in brackets in these sentences and rewrite the underlined passages. Add the appropriate preposition if necessary.

At first the class didn't really want to read Shakespeare's tragedy "Macbeth". (be keen)
At first the class wasn't keen on reading Shakespeare's tragedy "Macbeth".

After reading the opening scene, the students thought it absolutely necessary to go through that important scene again. (insist) [1]

_____

The teacher translated many passages of the play into modern English. He didn't want his class to lose interest. (prevent) [2]

_____

Did the witches warn Macbeth so that he wouldn't commit more murders? (prevent) [3]

_____

Luke is a very good actor. (be clever) [4]

_____

Harry <u>finds it difficult to learn</u> Macbeth's first monologue by heart. (have difficulty) [5]

_____

Actor Alec Thimble never <u>wanted to tell</u> journalists how long he took to learn the role of Macbeth. (like the idea) [6]

_____

For years Alfred Masterman has tried to play the main part in a Stratford production of "Macbeth". He has <u>now got</u> the part. (succeed) [7]

_____

The producer <u>thinks it's absolutely necessary that</u> young actors <u>take</u> fencing lessons. (insist) [8]

_____

16 Gerund or Infinitive – Put the verbs in brackets into the correct form (gerund or infinitive). Add an appropriate preposition if necessary.

A visit to Stratford

At the end of term my friend Martin suggested ___*going*___ (going/to go) to Stratford, Shakespeare's birthplace. Looking back I must admit _____ [1] (going/to go) to Stratford, Shakespeare's birthplace, was quite a good idea. But I wouldn't fancy _____ [2] (visiting/to visit) the place in summer again. You just cannot imagine the millions of tourists from all over the world _____ [3] (coming/to come) together in that tiny village in Warwickshire! Every day busloads of "culture vultures" arrive who must have been told that Stratford is worth _____ [4] (visiting/to visit).
When we arrived it wasn't easy _____ [5] (finding/to find) a place to stay. As we hadn't anticipated _____ [6] (being/to be) in the midst of thousands of tourists we hadn't booked a hotel room in advance. I hate _____ [7] (saying/to say) it, but that was rather stupid of us! How could we not have thought of that!? The only thing I can say is that from one day to another Martin and I just felt like _____ [8] (packing/to pack) our cases and _____ [9] (leaving/to leave).
Anyway, the first thing we did in Stratford was to stop at the tourist information office _____ [10] (trying/to try) to book a room for us. The people there were very helpful, but they told us it was extremely hard _____ [11] (finding/to find) a place if you hadn't booked in advance.

They phoned several hotels and tried _____¹² (squeezing/to squeeze) us in somewhere. But – no luck. They finally suggested _____¹³ (driving/ to drive) up and down the streets – we might be lucky and find a B & B (bed and breakfast). Believe it or not, after three hours we were about to give up _____¹⁴ (looking/to look) when – against all odds – we succeeded _____¹⁵ (finding/to find) a nice room in the house of the Taylors a bit outside of Stratford.

The Taylors told us it was no use _____¹⁶ (queuing/to queue) for tickets for the performance at eight o'clock. Hundreds would try _____¹⁷ (getting/to get) one for the day. But it might be worthwhile _____¹⁸ (trying/to try) a matinee which started at four in the afternoon. We were just about to leave and try our luck when Zoe, the daughter of the Taylors, arrived. During her school holidays she worked as an extra in several plays and she remembered _____¹⁹ (seeing/to see) a notice that there were still a few tickets for students available for the same day. So we dashed off – and we did manage _____²⁰ (getting/to get) in! The view was a bit obstructed – but we enjoyed _____²¹ (listening/to listen) to the poetic passages in "A Midsummer Night's Dream"!

If you ever think of going to Stratford – which you should – you must avoid _____²² (coming/to come) in the main season. You ought to consider _____²³ (coming/to come) at the beginning of the season if you can manage that. I'm sure you will be able _____²⁴ (enjoying/to enjoy) your stay even more than we did when we were there in the middle of August.

17 Gerund with subject of its own – Replace the *that*-clause by a different construction. In some sentences the gerund has a subject of its own.

Jacob and Emily want to see a play at the Royal Shakespeare Company.

Emily's parents don't object to the fact that Emily goes out with Jacob.
Emily's parents don't object to Emily('s) going out with Jacob.

To earn some extra money Emily works in the Swan's Nest hotel in Stratford. Emily doesn't mind that she works [1] as a chambermaid.

_____

Jacob dislikes it that Emily works [2]. They can't go to tonight's performance of "Romeo and Juliet" together.

_____

Emily doesn't mind that they cannot go [3] tonight.

_____

Jacob hopes that he will get [4] two tickets for tomorrow's matinee performance.

_____

Eventually he manages to get two seats with slightly obstructed view. He doesn't mind that they have to sit [5] behind a pillar.

_____

Then Jacob suddenly remembers that Emily complained [6] the last time he bought two of those cheap tickets.

_____

So he goes back to the ticket office: "I'm sorry that I must return [7] these tickets. I'm afraid my girlfriend won't like them."

_____

He tells Emily about what happened and adds, "I hope you don't mind that I didn't buy [8] any. I'll take you out for a nice meal instead."

_____

Emily is delighted and suggests that they dress up [9] for the occasion.

_____

She insists that Jacob doesn't turn up [10] in an open shirt, so she buys him a tie and the couple enter the restaurant in their best formal outfit.

_____

Modale Hilfsverben • Modal Auxiliaries

Verben werden im Englischen in drei Gruppen eingeteilt:

- Vollverben,
- Hilfsverben (*to be, to do, to have*) und
- modale Hilfsverben (*can, may, must, will, shall*).

Die modalen Hilfsverben werden zuweilen auch als „unvollständige" Hilfsverben (*defective auxiliaries*) bezeichnet, da sie keine Infinitivform und kein Partizip haben und nicht alle Zeitformen bilden können.

1 Form und Bildung

- Die modalen Hilfsverben haben für alle Personen **nur eine Form** (kein -s in der 3. Person Singular).

  The government <u>can</u> help the poor.
  All governments <u>can</u> help the poor.
  You, too, <u>can</u> help the poor.

- Auf modale Hilfsverben **folgt** der **Infinitiv ohne** *to*.

  Farmers <u>must</u> <u>produce</u> more food.

- **Frage** und **Verneinung** werden **ohne** *do / does / did* gebildet.

  <u>Can</u> we <u>achieve</u> an equal distribution of our wealth?

- Bestimmte **Zeitformen** (*will-future, present perfect, past perfect*) von modalen Hilfsverben werden mithilfe eines **Ersatzverbs** gebildet.

  We <u>will</u> <u>have to</u> solve the problem of overpopulation soon.

- Die modalen Hilfsverben können ein **direktes Objekt** nur **mithilfe eines Vollverbs anschließen**.

  Private initiative <u>can</u> <u>improve</u> <u>the living conditions</u> in many poor countries.

1.1 Übersicht über die modalen Hilfsverben und ihre Ersatzformen

Present tense	Past tense	Conditional	Substitute
I can (*können*)	I could	I could I could have	to be able to
I may (*dürfen*)	–	I might I might have	to be allowed to
I must (*müssen*)	–	–	to have to
I shall (*sollen*)	–	I should I should have	to be to
I will (*wollen*)	I would	I would I would have	to want/wish to

1.2 *can* als Beispiel für ein Modalverb in allen Zeiten

Tense	Positive form	Negative form
Present tense	I can help.	I can't help./I cannot help.
Will-future	I'll be able to help.	I won't be able to help.
Past tense	I could help. I was able to help.	I couldn't help. I wasn't able to help.
Present Perfect	I have been able to help.	I haven't been able to help.
Past Perfect	I had been able to help.	I hadn't been able to help.
Conditional	I could help. I would be able to help.	I couldn't help. I wouldn't be able to help.
Conditional perfect	I could have helped. I would have been able to help.	I couldn't have helped. I wouldn't have been able to help.

2 Gebrauch

2.1 *can / could* (‚können') – Ersatzverb: *to be able to*

can /could wird verwendet zum Ausdruck der

- **Möglichkeit** *(it is possible that)*,

  Do you think we <u>can</u> ask our headmaster to help us raise money for homeless people?
  Glaubst du, wir können unseren Schulleiter bitten, uns zu helfen, Geld für Obdachlose zu sammeln?

- **Fähigkeit** *(to be able to)*,

  I <u>can</u> tell you as soon as I've talked to him.
  I'<u>ll be able to</u> tell you after the break at 10.

- **Erlaubnis** *(to be allowed to)*.

  Last year students <u>couldn't</u> sell (= <u>weren't allowed to</u> sell) Xmas cards to raise money for their school-leaving celebration.

could kann sowohl *past tense* von *can* (‚konnte') sein als auch *conditional* (‚könnte').

2.2 *may / might* (‚dürfen') – Ersatzverb: *to be allowed to*

may /might wird verwendet zum Ausdruck der

- **Erlaubnis** *(to be allowed)*,

  <u>May</u> we <u>come</u> with you?

- **Vermutung** *(perhaps = ‚vielleicht')*,

  The headmaster <u>may</u> not <u>be</u> in his office.

- **geringen Wahrscheinlichkeit** (‚könnte').

  It <u>might help</u> if all of us went to see the headmaster.

2.3 *must* (‚müssen') – Ersatzverb: *to have to*

must wird verwendet zum Ausdruck der

- **Notwendigkeit** *(to have to)*,

  We <u>must try</u> to get the permission for the bazaar.

- **Gewissheit** *(to be sure /certain)*.

  There <u>must be</u> some way to convince the others that we're only trying to help those poor people.
  Es muss eine Möglichkeit geben, die anderen davon zu überzeugen, dass wir den Armen nur helfen wollen.

2.4 will/would ('wollen') – Ersatzverben: *to want, to wish, to desire*

will/would wird verwendet zum Ausdruck

- einer **Aufforderung, Bitte** (*to want to*),

The headmaster said, "Will you please sit down over there?"

- der **Entschlossenheit** (*to [not] want to*).

With time people get used to suffering, but we won't (= but we don't want to).
Mit der Zeit gewöhnen sich Menschen an das Leid, aber wir nicht (= aber wir wollen uns nicht daran gewöhnen).

2.5 shall/should ('sollen') – Ersatzverben: *to be to, to want*

shall/should wird verwendet zum Ausdruck

- einer **Mahnung** (*to be to*),

The rich shall help the poor.

- eines **Vorschlags** (*to want to*).

Shall I tell you what a poor peasant's day is really like? (= Do you want me to tell you …)
Soll ich Ihnen sagen, wie der Tag eines armen Kleinbauern wirklich aussieht?

3 Vertiefung

3.1 must not/need not

- *must not/mustn't* ('nicht dürfen') drückt ein **Verbot** aus.

We mustn't forget the poor people in developing countries.
Wir dürfen die Armen in den Entwicklungsländern nicht vergessen.

- *need not/needn't* ('nicht müssen') drückt das **Fehlen eines Zwangs** oder **einer Notwendigkeit** aus.

We needn't go to a developing country ourselves to know about the misery of the poor.
Wir brauchen nicht selbst in ein Entwicklungsland zu gehen, um über das Elend der Armen Bescheid zu wissen.

Die deutsche Wendung ‚du musst nicht/du brauchst nicht' kann nur durch *you need not/ you don't have to* wiedergegeben werden.

3.2 Deutsches ‚sollen'

- ‚Sollen' wird zum Ausdruck eines **Ratschlags** oder einer **Verpflichtung** durch *should* oder *ought to* wiedergegeben.

Social workers agree that immigrant families <u>should</u> get more support to facilitate their integration into the new society.
Sozialarbeiter sind der Meinung, dass Einwandererfamilien mehr Unterstützung bekommen <u>sollten</u>, um ihre Eingliederung in die neue Gesellschaft zu erleichtern.

- ‚Sollen' wird im Sinne einer **Weitergabe einer Information** durch *to be said to* wiedergegeben.

Young foreigners <u>are said to</u> get into trouble with the police more often.
Junge Ausländer <u>sollen</u> öfter Schwierigkeiten mit der Polizei haben.

- ‚Sollen' wird in der **Einleitung einer Frage** durch *shall* wiedergegeben.

This is a prejudice. <u>Shall</u> we go and see how young immigrants really live in our country?
Das ist ein Vorurteil. <u>Sollen</u> wir uns mal ansehen, wie junge Einwanderer wirklich leben in unserem Land?

- ‚Sollen' wird im Sinne einer **Weitergabe einer Anweisung** durch *to be to* wiedergegeben.

When you find out about their real situation you <u>are to</u> tell your classmates what you've seen.
Wenn du ihre wahren Lebensumstände kennst, <u>sollst</u> du deinen Klassenkameraden sagen, was du erfahren hast.

4 Übungen

18 Tenses – Complete the sentences with the information given in the heading. Make sure to choose the right tense for the modal auxiliary.

Jenny Shillingford is expecting her second baby. She and her husband Terry have decided that Jenny will give up work for some time in order to look after their baby.

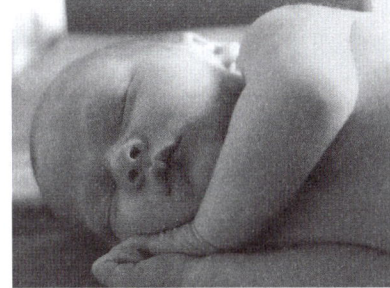

Jenny can look after her baby.

0   If she had more time,
    Jenny could look after her baby.

1   As soon as she'll stay at home _____

2 Since she's given up work _____

3 If she gives up work, _____

4 If she gave up work, _____

5 Ever since her mother has offered help _____

Jenny and her husband must cope with less money.

6 When they had their first baby _____

7 Since they have been married _____

8 For the next two years or so _____

9 If she gives up work, _____

10 If she went on working, _____

19 Negations – Put into the negative.

0 Terry must paint the baby's new cradle.
   Terry needn't paint the baby's new cradle. _____

1 Jenny and Terry have had to change a lot since the baby was born.

   _____

2 Jenny must get her baby daughter to bed before seven.

   _____

3 She must wash up all the baby bottles.

   _____

4 Last week she had to change the baby's nappies seven times a day.

   _____

5 When Jenny and Terry get a baby-sitter they'll have to pay her in advance.

   _____

6 When the baby cries Jenny must answer at once.

   _____

7 Next week Jenny and Terry will have to buy a new baby pram.

   _____

20 Negations – Put the headings into the negative and use this information to complete the sentences, choosing the correct tense for the modal auxiliary.

I must cope with my full-time job and bring up my children at the same time.

0 When I had my first baby *I didn't have to cope with my full-time job and bring up my children at the same time.*

1 In the next couple of months _____

   _____

2 If we didn't need the money, _____

   _____

Managers can afford to lose qualified female staff.

3 In future _____

   _____

4 Even in the past _____

   _____

5 Since the Japanese competition has been getting stiffer _____

   _____

6 In times of an economic slump _____

   _____

21 German 'sollen' – Fill in the gaps, using the following modal verbs. Please note that sometimes more than one answer is possible.

> be to – ought to – shall – should

What _____*shall we do*_____ (we, do) about all those poor people who haven't got a home to go to? The government _____[1] (be) more concerned about the increasing number of homeless people. Today it _____[2] (not, be) necessary for poor people to sleep rough, in trees or even dustbins. Shopkeepers say homeless people _____[3] (not, see) walking the streets of the city centre begging for money. The police _____[4] (do) more patrolling.
Unsympathetic people usually say, the homeless _____[5] (be) working instead of walking through the streets all day and hanging around in

underground stations. But how _____ ⁶ (we, solve) the problem of the homeless? _____ ⁷ (we, send) them all away? Where _____ ⁸ they go? How – in times of economic recession – _____ ⁹ (the city, provide) shelter, clothing and food? A new soup kitchen _____ ¹⁰ (build) near the Embankment. The town council decided on this yesterday. I'm convinced that everybody _____ ¹¹ (make) some financial contribution, that we all _____ ¹² (help) those in need.

22 Translation – Translate into English.

1 Darf ich Ihre Aufmerksamkeit auf ein aktuelles Problem richten: die Beschäftigung illegaler Einwanderer als Haushaltshilfen *(domestic helpers)*.

2 Selbst bekannte US-Politiker sollen illegale Einwanderer z. B. als Kindermädchen beschäftigt haben.

3 Natürlich dürfen Ausländer als Haushaltshilfen beschäftigt werden; übrigens darf man sie nicht „Diener" nennen.

4 Der Arbeitgeber muss sicherstellen, dass er nur Ausländer mit einer Arbeitserlaubnis beschäftigt.

5 Deshalb sollte man die Dokumente einsehen, bevor man jemanden beschäftigt.

6 Natürlich ist Sozialversicherung zu zahlen.

7 In den letzten Jahren konnten amerikanische Ehepaare einfach kein Kindermädchen auf dem Arbeitsmarkt finden.

8 Sie waren daher äußerst zufrieden, als sie schließlich eine Einwanderin beschäftigen konnten.

9 Außerdem war die Arbeitskraft billig: Illegale Arbeiter können natürlich nicht denselben Lohn wie legale Arbeiter erwarten.

10 Mehr als ein Politiker hätte im Amt bleiben können, wenn er nicht eine illegale Haushaltshilfe beschäftigt hätte.

Indirekte Rede • Reported Speech

Die indirekte Rede wird verwendet, um möglichst getreu und objektiv das wiederzugeben, was ein anderer gesagt hat. Damit der Berichtende deutlich machen kann, dass er etwas wiedergibt, wofür er nicht verantwortlich ist, distanziert er sich gewissermaßen von der ursprünglichen Äußerung. Im Deutschen geschieht das durch die Verwendung des Konjunktivs (meist Konjunktiv I), im Englischen durch die Verwendung einer anderen Zeit als im Original.

1   Gebrauch

In indirekter (berichtender) Rede gibt man wieder, **was jemand gesagt, gefragt** oder **befohlen** hat.

Als **Einleitungsverben** der indirekten Rede *(reporting verbs)* stehen z. B. zur Verfügung:

to add	to emphasize	to mention	to state
to agree	to go on	to point out	to tell
to answer	to know	to remark	to think
to continue	to make clear	to say	to want to know

Die Pronomina, eventuell die Zeitstufe und die Adverbien der direkten Rede verändern sich in der indirekten Rede wie folgt:

1.1   Pronomina • Pronouns

Die Pronomina verändern sich wie im Deutschen.

	Direkte Rede	Indirekte Rede
Personalpronomen	I, you, we, you	he, she, they
Possessivpronomen	my, your, our, your	his, her, their
Demonstrativpronomen	this, these	that, those

1.2 Zeiten

Steht das **Einleitungsverb der Rede im** *present tense, present perfect* oder *will-future*, so wird die **Zeit**, die in der direkten Rede verwendet wurde, **nicht geändert**.

Direkte Rede	Indirekte Rede
Judy <u>says</u>, "I <u>don't like</u> hamburgers very much."	Judy <u>says</u> (that) she <u>doesn't like</u> hamburgers very much.

Steht das **Einleitungsverb der Rede im** *past tense*, dann wird die Zeit, die in der direkten Rede verwendet wurde, um **eine Zeitstufe zurückversetzt**. Man spricht von Zeitenverschiebung (= *backshift of tenses*). [siehe unten, Abschnitt 2.1]

Direkte Rede	Indirekte Rede
Judy <u>said</u>, "I <u>don't like</u> hamburgers very much."	Judy <u>said</u> (that) she <u>didn't like</u> hamburgers very much.

1.3 Besonderheiten bei der Zeichensetzung und Übersetzung

- Vor der indirekten Rede steht im Englischen **kein Komma**.

  Judy said she didn't like hamburgers very much.

- In der **deutschen Übersetzung** wird in der Regel der **Konjunktiv** verwendet. Nur wenn man etwas sicher weiß oder von einer Sache überzeugt ist, wird im Deutschen der Indikativ gebraucht.

  Judy sagte, sie <u>esse</u> Hamburger nicht besonders gerne.

2 Vertiefung

2.1 Zeitenverschiebung • The Backshift of Tenses

Aussagesätze

Present tense in der direkten Rede **wird zu** *past tense* in der indirekten Rede.

Direkte Rede	Indirekte Rede
Tony: "I'<u>m</u> a vegetarian and I never <u>eat</u> meat."	Tony said that he <u>was</u> a vegetarian and that he never <u>ate</u> meat.

Present tense in der direkten Rede **kann unverändert bleiben**, wenn eine **allgemeingültige Aussage** gemacht wird (Naturgesetz, Gewohnheit, Eigenschaft).

Direkte Rede	Indirekte Rede
Professor Harvey stated: "The chemical name of vitamin A <u>is</u> retinol."	Professor Harvey stated (that) the chemical name of vitamin A <u>is</u> retinol.

Past tense in der direkten Rede **wird zu *past perfect*** in der indirekten Rede.

Direkte Rede	Indirekte Rede
Sally: "I <u>started</u> work at seventeen."	Sally said that she <u>had started</u> work at seventeen.

Present perfect in der direkten Rede **wird zu *past perfect*** in der indirekten Rede.

Direkte Rede	Indirekte Rede
Tony: "I <u>haven't eaten</u> in an Indian restaurant for months."	Tony said that he <u>hadn't eaten</u> in an Indian restaurant for months.

Will-future in der direkten Rede **wird zu *conditional*** in der indirekten Rede.

Direkte Rede	Indirekte Rede
"Fred <u>will be</u> a cook soon."	He said that Fred <u>would be</u> a cook soon.

Fragen

Fragen werden in der indirekten Rede eingeleitet durch *to ask, to want to know* und *to wonder*. Das **Fragepronomen** der direkten Rede wird in der indirekten Rede **wiederholt**.

Direkte Rede	Indirekte Rede
He said, "<u>Where</u> is the nearest restaurant?"	He <u>asked where</u> the nearest restaurant was.

Steht in der direkten Rede kein Fragepronomen, so werden *if* oder *whether* eingesetzt.

Direkte Rede	Indirekte Rede
"Is fast food healthy?"	She <u>asked if (whether)</u> fast food was healthy.

Aufforderungen, Ratschläge und Befehle

Aufforderungen werden – je nach Sinngehalt – durch **Verb + Objekt + (*not* +) Infinitiv** wiedergegeben. Durch die Wahl des entsprechenden **Einleitungsverbs** drückt man aus, ob es sich um eine **höfliche Aufforderung** (*to ask*), einen **Rat** (*to advise*) oder einen strengeren **Befehl** (*to tell, to order, to command*) handelt.

Direkte Rede	Indirekte Rede
She said, "Please get me another drink."	She <u>asked</u> him <u>to get</u> her another drink.
	Sie bat ihn, …
He said, "<u>Don't eat</u> so many chocolates, Sandra!"	He <u>advised</u> Sandra <u>not to eat</u> so many chocolates.
	Er riet Sandra, …
He said, "<u>Drink up</u>, Tom!"	He <u>told</u> Tom <u>to drink up</u>.
	Er forderte Tom auf, …

2.2 Adverbiale

Adverbiale der Zeit (*adverbs and adverbial phrases of time*) verändern sich so:

Direkte Rede →	Indirekte Rede
today	that day
yesterday	the day before
the day before yesterday	two days before
tomorrow	the next day / the following day
the day after tomorrow	in two days' time, two days later
next week / year etc.	the following week / year etc.
a month / year ago etc.	a month / year before etc.
now	then

Das **Adverbial des Ortes** (*adverb of place*) *here* wird in der indirekten Rede zu *there*. Steht *there* in der direkten Rede, so bleibt es in der indirekten Rede unverändert.

2.3 Hilfsverben • Auxiliaries

Stehen diese **Hilfsverben** in der direkten Rede, so werden sie **unverändert** in die indirekte Rede übernommen: *could, had better, might, ought, should, used to, would*.

Direkte Rede	Indirekte Rede
Sue: "I <u>might</u> go on a diet after the holidays."	Sue said (that) she <u>might</u> go on a diet after the holidays.

Das Hilfsverb *must* bildet eine Ausnahme. Es wird in der indirekten Rede durch *to have to* unter Berücksichtigung der entsprechenden Zeitverschiebung wiedergegeben.

Direkte Rede:	Indirekte Rede:
Sue: "I <u>must</u> eat less, my dear!"	Sue said (that) she <u>had to eat</u> less.

3 Übungen

23 Using Reported Speech

The bad boy of burgers

Environmentalists and nutritional experts had heavily criticized the fast food restaurant chain BIG BURGER *because of the nutritional value of its meals, its wasteful packaging etc. The management of the company feared that due to the harsh criticism customers might stay away, so they decided to invite journalists to a press conference to put the facts straight. The manager, Harold E. Holstein, welcomed his guests in the headquarters of his company and said:*

"Food hygiene and quality have always been important to our company. There has been much debate recently regarding the quality of meat used in the fast service restaurant industry. I can assure you that only prime cuts of lean forequarter and flank are used for our beef hamburgers. We use no additives; no fillers, no binders, no flavour enhancers: just 100 % pure beef. Our beef comes from EU approved European suppliers. Every consignment of beef is subject to a total of 36 quality control checks. If a consignment should fail on any one check – it will be rejected by BIG BURGER. In addition, a Ministry of Agriculture representative visits the plant weekly to monitor its hygiene standards.

BIG BURGER has always been very conscious of all issues relating to the environment, including unnecessary outer packaging. Two years ago our management took the decision to invest in the launch of environmentally sound packaging solutions. Our packaging supplier was instructed to use the best sustainable, recyclable and at the same time food-safe alternative. This changeover was completed last year. So all BIG BURGER packaging is plant-based and biodegradable. This change in the manufacturing process does not affect the quality of the packaging."

Doug Dinsdale attended the press conference for the Evening Post. Afterwards he writes his article for tomorrow's paper. Put the words of the manager into reported speech using as many reporting verbs as possible (point out / make it clear / emphasize / continue / go on / add etc.). Start like this:

At the press conference the manager of BIG BURGER said food hygiene and quality had always been important to his company. He told the journalists ...

24 Using Reported Speech

As it had been said that BIG BURGER was involved with the destruction of rain forests of Central and South America to raise cattle for hamburgers, BIG BURGER manager Harold E. Holstein also referred to this criticism and their efforts at environmental protection and waste management.

"Our restaurants only use suppliers who document that their beef has come from long-established cattle ranches – not rain forest land. Rain forest destruction threatens the well-being of the environment. BIG BURGER has no part in it. Nowhere in the world does BIG BURGER's use of beef threaten the tropical rain forests. The company will continue to adapt policies and practices which are necessary to protect the global environment. This includes researching ways of saving resources such as fossil fuels and water when producing meat and investing in methods to minimize air and water pollution.

Another issue that has always been important to us is effective waste management. In this area, recycling has become a vital part because it provides a way to eliminate items from the waste stream. BIG BURGER is already the largest user of biodegradable and recyclable packaging material in the quick service restaurant industry but our customers need to contribute, too. We are currently running pilot schemes at several restaurants in the Croydon area where customers are asked to separate their waste and put food remains in one bin and recyclable cartons in another. A similar scheme already operates successfully in many of our US restaurants. We will continue to ensure that we are serving our customers in the best and safest way while keeping environmental impact as low as possible."

When Doug returned from the press conference he had lunch with his colleague Andrew Shepperton, who wanted to know what the manager had said.

What did the manager say about ...

0   ... what sort of suppliers they use?

He said that they only used suppliers who documented that their beef had come from long-established cattle ranches – not rain forest land.

1   ... the destruction of the rain forests?

2   ... BIG BURGER's part in the destruction?

3   ... BIG BURGER's use of beef and the rain forests?

4   ... the future policies and practices of the company with reference to the environment?

5   ... their research and investments?

6   ... about the role of recycling?

7   ... the use of packaging material in their restaurants?

8   ... any pilot schemes?

9   ... customers' contributions to reduce the waste?

10   ... US practices?

11   ... future policies?

25 Reported Speech – Tenses

Help me – I'm too fat!

Marie-Ann Winford went to see a nutritional expert and told her about her weight problem.

"I've come to you for help. I think I'm too fat.
I don't want to look like a model, but I want to lose
about three stone and get back to the weight I was when I married.

The trouble is, I lack will-power. I've tried everything, from calorie-counting to appetite suppressants. But nothing helps. I start a diet, but a few days later, I'll crave for a bar of chocolate or a handful of biscuits, and it all goes downhill again.

I can't keep anything in the house that might tempt me – so the whole family is on a diet, too, whether they like it or not. My husband, Anthony, and my children all eat the same food as me: salads, low-calorie soup, low-fat spreads, diet lemonade and skimmed milk.

Only yesterday my husband said, 'I like you the way you are!' But I sometimes wish he'd give me more encouragement. It takes such a lot of effort to lose just a few pounds. I think he should support me a little more. But no! Last week he brought home a box of chocolates. Within half an hour I had eaten the lot. I was thoroughly miserable and blamed him – he knows I can't resist sweets when they're in front of me. What can I do?"

Put into reported speech, making any necessary changes. Start like this:

Marie–Ann Winford **told** *the nutritional expert (that)* **she had come** *to her for help. ...*

26 Reported Speech – Questions

When Marie-Ann had finished the nutritional expert asked her a few questions.

0   How old are you?
1   How long have you been married?
2   How old are your children?
3   Do you go to work?
4   What did you do before you got married?
5   Why do you want to lose weight?
6   When did you first put on weight?
7   What food do you like best?
8   Do you eat in between meals?
9   When do you eat your last meal of the day?
10 Do you have any financial worries?
11 Will you go back to work when your children are older?
12 Do your children complain about "health food"?
13 Are they allowed to eat sweets in between meals?

In the evening her husband Anthony asks Marie-Ann what the expert had wanted to know. Give Marie-Ann's answers:
"The expert wanted to know / asked / inquired / wondered etc. ...

0   *... how old I was."*
1   _____
2   _____
3   _____
4   _____
5   _____
6   _____
7   _____
8   _____
9   _____
10 _____
11 _____
12 _____
13 _____

27 Reported Speech – Advice

This is the advice Marie-Ann received from the nutritional expert:

0 Get information about the nutritional value of foods and drinks!
1 Eat enough of the right food!
2 Take up exercise every day!
3 Avoid eating too much fat!
4 Cook vegetables carefully!
5 Don't buy any sweets!
6 Eat lots of fresh fruit!
7 Drink plenty of water!
8 Keep away from the fridge!
9 Eat a plate of raw vegetables every day!
10 Avoid artificially coloured and flavoured food!
11 Don't teach your children unhealthy eating habits!
12 Don't worry about your children's or husband's weight!
13 Replace white flour and white rice with whole-grain products!

Marie-Ann tells Anthony what the expert told her to do. Complete her answers:
"She told / advised me …

0   *… to get information about the nutritional value of foods."*

1   _____

2   _____

3   _____

4   _____

5   _____

6   _____

7   _____

8   _____

9   _____

10 _____

11 _____

12 _____

13 _____

Der Infinitiv • The Infinitive

1 Form und Bildung

Es werden folgende Formen des Infinitivs unterschieden:

1.1 Aktiv

Infinitiv Präsens Aktiv *(present active infinitive)*	to call
Infinitiv Perfekt Aktiv *(perfect active infinitive)*	to have called
Verlaufsform des Infinitivs *(progressive infinitive)*	(to) be calling

1.2 Passiv

Infinitiv Präsens Passiv *(present passive infinitive)*	to be called
Infinitiv Perfekt Passiv *(perfect passive infinitive)*	to have been called

2 Gebrauch

Der Infinitiv hat im Satz zwei Haupt-
funktionen:

- **Subjekt** des Satzes

To study modern languages has become
an essential part of people's vocational
qualifications.
*Moderne Sprachen zu lernen (= Das Erlernen
moderner Sprachen) ist ein wesentlicher Teil
der beruflichen Qualifikation der Menschen
geworden.*

• **adverbiale Bestimmung**	Heinrich Schliemann took only few weeks <u>to learn</u> another language. *H. S. brauchte nur wenige Wochen, bis er eine weitere Sprache gelernt hatte (…, [um] eine weitere Sprache zu erlernen).*

3   Vertiefung

3.1   Infinitiv mit *to*

Infinitiv mit *to* nach Substantiven, Verben, Adjektiven und Zahlenangaben

Der Infinitiv mit *to* steht nach:

- **Substantiven, die einen Zweck ausdrücken** (*plan, wish, attempt* etc.),

  Scotland has made an <u>attempt to ban</u> the physical punishment of children.
  Schottland hat einen Versuch gemacht, die körperliche Züchtigung von Kindern zu verbieten.

- **Verben, die einen Wunsch** oder **eine Absicht ausdrücken** (*to expect, to want, would like* etc.),

  England and Wales <u>would like to change</u> their laws in line with the Scottish plan.
  England und Wales würden ihre Gesetze gerne nach dem schottischen Vorbild ändern.

- **Adjektiven**, die **als Teil des Prädikats** gebraucht werden (*certain, hard, difficult, ready* etc.),

  Supporters of the plan believe that some countries will find it <u>difficult to follow</u> Scotland's initiative.
  Die Anhänger des Plans glauben, dass es einige Länder schwer haben werden, dem Beispiel Schottlands zu folgen.

- **Ordnungszahlen** und **Superlativen** (*the first, the last, the best, the only one* etc.).

  Sweden was <u>the first</u> country <u>to ban</u> corporal punishment in 1979.
  Schweden war das erste Land, das 1979 die Prügelstrafe verbot.
  [dt. Übersetzung = Relativsatz!]

Infinitiv mit *to* anstelle von Gliedsätzen

Der Infinitiv mit *to* steht anstelle

- eines **Relativsatzes**,

This could be the law to show people that smacking is not an appropriate means of education.
Dies könnte das Gesetz sein, das den Menschen klar macht, dass körperliche Züchtigung kein geeignetes Mittel der Erziehung ist.

- eines **Finalsatzes** (Zweck),

Denmark, Finland, Norway and Austria have already changed their laws to make the beating of children illegal.
Dänemark, Finnland, Norwegen und Österreich haben ihre Gesetze bereits geändert, um die körperliche Züchtigung von Kindern zu verbieten.

- eines **indirekten Fragesatzes**.

The Department of Health still doesn't know when to submit this new bill to Parliament.
Das Gesundheitsministerium weiß noch nicht, wann es dieses neue Gesetz dem Parlament vorlegt.

3.2 Infinitiv ohne *to*

Der Infinitiv ohne *to* steht nach:

- **modalen Hilfsverben** *(can, may, shall, will, must)*,

When they are 18 British sixth form students may take their A-levels.
Mit 18 können britische Oberstufenschüler ihr Abitur machen.

- **Verben der sinnlichen Wahrnehmung** *(to see, to hear* etc.), um auszudrücken, dass ein Geschehen oder eine Folge von Handlungen abgeschlossen ist;

The candidates saw the supervisor enter the room and they heard him say that they had 3 hours to do the test paper.
Die Prüflinge sahen, wie der Aufsichtführende den Raum betrat und sie hörten ihn sagen, sie hätten drei Stunden Zeit, um die Prüfungsaufgabe zu bearbeiten.

- wenn man den **Verlauf einer Handlung besonders betonen** möchte, kann man auch das **Partizip Präsens** (*ing*-form) verwenden;

The supervisor looked up now and again and saw the candidates working hard.
Der Aufsichtführende blickte ab und zu auf und sah, wie die Prüflinge fleißig arbeiteten.

- **Verben des Veranlassens** und **Zulassens** *(to make, to let).*

Teachers of science ask themselves how they can <u>make</u> more students <u>take</u> physics at A-level.

Die Lehrer der naturwissenschaftlichen Fächer fragen sich, wie sie mehr Schüler dazu bringen können, das Abitur im Fach Physik abzulegen (= Physik als Abiturfach zu wählen).

3.3   Objekt + Infinitiv-Konstruktion

Direktes Objekt + Infinitiv
Das direkte Objekt ist sinngemäß das Subjekt der Infinitivkonstruktion.

More and more bank managers expect <u>their</u> <u>employees to speak</u> one or two European languages.

Immer mehr Bankmanager erwarten, dass ihre Mitarbeiter eine oder zwei europäische Sprachen können.

3.4   *with* + Infinitiv

- Die Konstruktion *with* + Infinitiv wird häufig verwendet, um die Begleitumstände *(accompanying circumstances)* oder die Gründe für eine Situation mitzuteilen.
  Deutsche Übersetzung: Kausalsatz (‚da', ‚weil')

<u>With</u> so many essays <u>to write</u> Marc didn't have any time to go out with Lena.

<u>Da</u> Marc so viele Aufsätze <u>schreiben musste,</u> hatte er keine Zeit, mit Lena auszugehen.

- Wenn die Konstruktion *with* + Infinitiv **mit einem eigenen Subjekt in einen vollständigen Hauptsatz** einbezogen wird, hat der Infinitiv den Sinn eines erläuternden Relativsatzes.
  Deutsche Übersetzung: Relativsatz

<u>With</u> <u>his brother Simon to help</u> him Marc felt more confident when doing his Latin translation.

Da er seinen Bruder Simon hatte, <u>der ihm helfen konnte,</u> fühlte sich Marc sicherer, wenn er seine lateinische Übersetzung anfertigte.

3.5   *for* + Infinitiv

for + Nomen / Pronomen + Infinitiv (= for-Konstruktion)
Deutsche Übersetzung: dass-Satz

It was quite normal <u>for</u> <u>the boys to help</u> each other with their homework.

Es war ganz normal, <u>dass</u> die Jungen sich bei ihren Hausaufgaben halfen.

3.6 Infinitiv im Passiv

Die Passivform des Infinitivs steht nach: *to be (there is), to leave, to remain*

Much <u>remains</u> <u>to be done</u> to make our educational system more effective.

<u>Es bleibt</u> *(ist) viel* <u>zu tun</u>, ...
[= im Deutschen Aktiv!]

3.7 Deutsches ‚lassen‘

Das deutsche Wort ‚lassen‘ kann zwei Bedeutungen haben:

- Unser Klassenlehrer lässt so manches mit sich machen. (= ‚zulassen‘, ‚erlauben‘)
- Der Direktor lässt die Klassensprecher zu sich kommen. (= ‚dazu bewegen‘, ‚veranlassen, dass sie kommen‘)

Die beiden unterschiedlichen Bedeutungen werden im Englischen durch verschiedenartige Konstruktionen wiedergegeben.

1 ‚zulassen‘

let + Objekt + Infinitv ohne *to* (‚jdm. erlauben, etwas zu tun‘, ‚zulassen, dass etwas geschieht‘)

Jenny still hasn't got over her cold yet. We'd better <u>let</u> <u>her</u> <u>stay</u> in bed for another day or two.

2 ‚veranlassen‘

- *make/have* + Objekt + Infinitiv ohne *to* (‚jdn. dazu bewegen oder zwingen, etwas zu tun‘, ‚veranlassen, dass etwas geschieht‘)

Mr Grieves <u>made</u> <u>the boys</u> <u>read</u> a play by Shakespeare.
Mr Grieves <u>*ließ*</u> *die Jungen ein Stück von Shakespeare* <u>*lesen*</u>.

Grieves will <u>have</u> <u>them</u> <u>act</u> the play next.
Demnächst <u>*wird*</u> *Grieves sie das Stück* <u>*spielen*</u> <u>*lassen*</u>.

- *have/get* + Objekt + *past participle*

Your backpack looks like new again.
– Yes, I <u>had</u> <u>it</u> <u>repaired</u> last week.
Ja, ich <u>*ließ*</u> *ihn letzte Woche* <u>*reparieren*</u>.

Beachte: *get* wird hauptsächlich in der Umgangssprache verwendet.

My camera doesn't work properly any more.
– Well, why don't you <u>get</u> <u>it</u> <u>repaired</u>?
Also, warum <u>*lässt*</u> *du sie nicht* <u>*reparieren*</u>?

4 Übungen

28 Object + infinitive construction – Complete the story by putting in a suitable object from Box A and a suitable infinitive from Box B (with *to* if necessary).

Box A: OBJECTS
employers – young pupils – her husband – his wife – our boy – managers – more and more parents – our child – rich parents – their son – the headmaster

Box B: VERBS
check – register – choose – decide – enjoy – go – hate – hire – oppose – leave – reconsider

Job applicants would like **managers to check** their qualifications rather than the place where they were educated.

The poor academic standard in some state schools has made _____ ¹ to send their children to a public school. Two of the most famous public schools are Eton and Harrow. Some parents ask _____ _____ ² their children shortly after they are born. Because of the high school fees, it is only possible for _____ _____ ³ Eton, Harrow or Winchester for the education of their children. Critics of private education argue that it makes _____ ⁴ applicants who were educated at a private school rather than those who are better qualified.

George Ellis of Northolt doesn't like the John Lille comprehensive school in his neighbourhood. He's told his wife he doesn't want _____ ⁵ there. Pauline Ellis dislikes the suggestion, so she has asked _____ ⁶ it. Her main argument against sending children to a boarding school is that the feeling of homesickness might make _____ ⁷ school despite all the facilities offered there. "Alright, alright, the teachers may be very good", Pauline Ellis told her husband George, "but will going to a public school make _____ ⁸ learning more than at a state school? I'll be quite candid with you, George. I don't want _____ ⁹ home at the age of 7 or 8 to go to prep school!" Mr Ellis felt a bit on edge. He hadn't expected _____ _____ ¹⁰ his idea of private education for Joshua so vigorously.

29 Infinitive with *to* or without *to*? – Fill in a suitable verb from this list and use the infinitive with or without *to*.

> attend – know – prepare – update – get ahead – meeting/meet – prove – write – go – sit –
> obtain – improve – participate – take

People who do not have any certificate of higher education often find it difficult _____¹ in their jobs. Employers often expect their employees _____² their knowledge in their respective professional areas. For anyone who needs better qualifications the Open University is definitely one of the best institution _____³ to. Even adults who have left school without qualifications are given the opportunity _____⁴ in higher education. There are also students at the Open University who do not wish _____⁵ a degree but who just want _____⁶ their education. As most students are in full-time employment they are not expected _____⁷ regular classes; they study at home in their own time. Students are taught by a combination of correspondence texts and online courses and they are asked _____⁸ texts and _____⁹ essays at home. To let students _____¹⁰ where they are and whether they are getting on alright they can get tuition at special study centres. On Saturdays, you can see Open University students _____¹¹ their tutors at colleges and universities when the ordinary students are not there. Students are not obliged _____¹² any exams _____¹³ that have finished a course successfully. But those who would like _____¹⁴ a BA Honours Degree for example require eight credits, which means they must have done four years at the Open University.

30 Infinitive: Active or Passive – Complete these sentences, using either an active or passive infinitive of the verbs in brackets.

Towards a new curriculum

Much remains _to be done_ (do) to make our educational system more effective. Both parents and politicians are convinced that with the rise of technology some aspects of teaching ought _____¹ (change). When the government published a White Paper on Education the teachers' unions complained that they ought _____² (ask) about their opinion first. Some teachers felt that they were usually the last _____³ (ask) their views. It was eventually agreed that because of the widespread use of calculators and computers subjects like long-division and logarithms should no longer _____⁴ (teach) in maths lessons. Not all parents' associations, though, wanted the curriculum _____⁵ (change) in this respect. Due to the enlargement of the EU the European nations have come closer together. Managers would like modern languages _____⁶ (teach) more than in the past. At an early age pupils ought _____⁷ (make/learn) at least two European languages, not only to enable a better understanding of other nations, but also in order _____⁸ (facilitate) business relations. In the field of learning modern languages Britain is not _____⁹ (find) among the best in Europe and much remains _____¹⁰ (desire) in this respect. It could be difficult for many teachers _____¹¹ (adapt) to the new curriculum and its requirements and regulations. Teachers will be told precisely what _____ _____¹² (teach) and pupils will be told what _____¹³ (learn). Parents, on the other hand, feel that not everything should be left to the government and the authorities _____¹⁴ (decide). Some parents, though, would prefer education _____¹⁵ (remain) in the hands of the local education authorities only – especially parents who do not know how _____¹⁶ (cope) with their offspring –, but most parents want _____¹⁷ (have) a say in educational matters.

31 German 'lassen' – Complete the sentences. Use the words in brackets, adding either *have*, *make*, or *let*. Sometimes you may need an object to form a proper English version of the German 'lassen'.

Educating Muriel

Muriel Reed _had herself registered_ (herself/register) as a student of the Open University. Muriel works as a secretary in the export department of the Orion chocolate factory in Bracknell. She left school at 16 and would like to get ahead in her job now, so she _____¹ (her name/put down) as a student of the management course offered by the Open University study centre in Slough. Her boss, Mr Linehan, encourages her efforts. As a responsible manager he knows it pays to _____² (the skills of the staff/update) regularly. About two years ago he even _____ _____³ (Muriel/attend) a special word processing training course during her normal working hours. When Muriel informed him about her new studies, Mr Linehan told her he would be prepared to _____

_____⁴ (go home) a bit earlier so that she could attend the online videoconference accompanying her managerial course.

When Muriel first went to Slough to register she had expected that the Open University people would _____⁵ (take) some sort of entrance test, but Brenda, the Open University representative, told her that they _____⁶ (anybody/start) and that no qualifications were needed. Brenda gave Muriel a pile of leaflets. "In these notes we _____ _____⁷ (you know) everything you need to follow Professor Hamilton's course successfully. He always _____⁸ (his students/read) three to four set books and _____⁹ (them/write) two or three essays per semester. But he doesn't _____¹⁰ (anybody/take) the final exam; he _____¹¹ (everybody/decide) for themselves."

32 Translating _with_ + infinitive – Translate into German.

0 **With** her son Joshua **to take** the admission examination to Winchester School soon, Mrs Ellis was worried about him.

Da ihr Sohn Joshua bald seine Aufnahmeprüfung an der Winchester School
machen würde, machte Frau Ellis sich Sorgen um ihn.

1 With only three months to go before the examination, Joshua felt rather nervous.

_____

_____

2 He was kept busy with all the revision work to do.

_____

_____

3 His father thought his son would feel rather lost with no one to support him; so he asked Mr Dewy, the old English teacher, to help Joshua.

_____

_____

4 Joshua's mother was convinced that he couldn't cope without someone to help him.

_____

_____

5   Mr Ellis hoped that Joshua would work hard with no thoughts about holidays to distract him from his efforts.

_____

_____

6   So for the next couple of months Joshua won't be a pupil with nothing to do. On the contrary.

_____

_____

7   If Joshua had extra tuition, he would have a greater chance of passing the admission examination than most of his classmates without anybody to help them.

_____

_____

33   Translating *for* + infinitive – Translate into German.

0   It is quite normal **for the Ellis' to help** Joshua with his homework.
Es ist ganz normal, dass die Ellis Joshua bei den Hausaufgaben helfen.

1   They are anxious for their boy to be accepted at Winchester.

_____

2   It's important for Joshua to be ready by June.

_____

3   It's not unusual for the College to increase its number of scholarships.

_____

4   It's essential for the standard of teaching at Winchester to have the best tutors available.

_____

34   *For* + infinitive – Rewrite the following sentences using a *for*-construction.

0   The boys helped each other with their homework. It was quite normal.
It was quite normal for the boys to help each other with their homework.

1   Many examination questions were too difficult. Lisa couldn't answer them.

_____

2   One question was extremely difficult. I don't think anybody could have answered it.

_____

3   Lisa must work harder. It would be good for her.

_____

4   She must start today. It's time.

_____

5   Her English essay was not good enough. The teacher didn't accept it.

_____

35 Using the *for*-construction – Fill each gap in the text by putting in the words in brackets. Be careful with the tenses.

Daniel Benteen was 14 years old and went to Westminster School. One night it was quite a _shock for his mate Ron to discover_ (shock/his mate Ron/discover) that Daniel had climbed out of the dormitory window onto the roof. It was not _____¹ (unusual/Daniel/try out) some tricks to entertain and impress the other boys. He could hardly _____ _____² (wait/Ron/wake up) the others and tell them. Although it was almost too _____³ (nerve-racking/the boys/watch) Daniel climbing round to the next window, they all gazed out. Knowing that it was _____⁴ (impossible/his mates/make) him come back, Daniel pretended to slip but eventually pulled himself up again.

He knew that they would _____⁵ (arrange/the janitor/come) and get him back in again and be reported to the headmaster. But he didn't mind. Actually, he was waiting _____⁶ (them/do) something, so that he could end his little trip with some sort of applause from the crowd.

It took five minutes _____⁷ (the janitor/arrive). The headmaster would be bound _____⁸ (arrange/his father/come) and see him. Daniel was sure his father would tell him off, but leave it at that. He didn't understand that in reality Daniel got into mischief not only to impress his mates, but also because he wanted to be taken away from that school and go back home again.

Die Partizipien • The Participles

Es werden zwei Arten von Partizipien unterschieden:
- das Partizip Präsens
- das Partizip Perfekt

1 Partizip Präsens • Present Participle

1.1 Form und Bildung

Infinitiv + -ing	As James was <u>driving</u> along a boring stretch of motorway, he felt very tired.

1.2 Gebrauch

Partizip Präsens wird verwendet:

- zur Bildung der **Verlaufsform** (to be + Partizip Präsens),

  Look at Joe Bloggs again, he <u>is</u> <u>driving</u> much too fast!

- in der Funktion eines **Adjektivs**, das ein Nomen näher bestimmt,

  The <u>driving</u> teenager.

- **anstelle eines Relativsatzes im Aktiv** [siehe auch S. 72],

  People <u>driving</u> <u>too fast</u> should be fined more heavily.
  Leute, die zu schnell fahren, sollten härter bestraft werden.

- zur **Verkürzung** eines **Adverbial-satzes** (hier: der Zeit) [siehe auch S. 72],

  <u>Riding the new Triumph model</u> Jeff completely forgot about the time.
  Als Jeff das neue Triumphmodell fuhr, vergaß er die Zeit völlig.

- nach **Verben der sinnlichen Wahr-nehmung** (to see, to hear etc.) [siehe auch Kapitel Infinitiv],

  I didn't <u>see</u> the two cars <u>crashing</u> into each other.
  Ich sah nicht, wie die zwei Autos zusammen-stießen.

- als Subjekt des Satzes = **Gerundium** [siehe auch Kapitel Gerundium].

  <u>Riding</u> a Harley Davidson is fun.
  Eine Harley Davidson zu fahren macht Spaß.

2 Partizip Perfekt • Past Participle

2.1 Form und Bildung

Infinitiv + *-ed, -d* bzw.
3. Form der unregelmäßigen Verben.

Yellow cabs often <u>driven</u> by coloured immigrants are a familiar sight in New York City.

2.2 Gebrauch

Das Partizip Perfekt wird verwendet:

- **anstelle eines Relativsatzes im Passiv** [siehe auch S. 71],

Many cars <u>driven</u> <u>by students</u> are old bangers.
Viele Autos, die von Studenten gefahren werden, sind alte Klapperkisten.

- **anstelle eines Adverbialsatzes** zur Bezeichnung einer vorzeitigen Handlung [siehe auch S. 73],

Having <u>driven</u> <u>for three hours</u>, James felt tired.
Nachdem James drei Stunden lang gefahren war, fühlte er sich müde.

- zur **Bildung des deutschen 'lassen'** (*have* + Objekt + Partizip) [siehe auch Kapitel Infinitiv].

"Your car looks like new again."
– "Yes, I <u>had</u> it <u>painted</u> last month."
„Ich <u>ließ</u> es letzten Monat <u>lackieren</u>."

Beachte: In der Umgangssprache wird häufig *get* anstelle von *have* verwendet.

"Why didn't you <u>get</u> it <u>repaired</u>, too?"
„Warum hast du es nicht auch <u>reparieren lassen</u>?"

3 Vertiefung

3.1 Satzverkürzung • Syntactic Compression

Das Partizip wird häufig zur Verkürzung von Sätzen verwendet, vor allem im schriftlichen Englisch. Man spricht von *syntactic compression*. Verkürzt werden:

Relativsätze • Relative Clauses

Aktivsätze werden mit dem **Partizip Präsens** verkürzt.

long version	shortened version
A new service station <u>which offers more facilities to drivers than the older stations</u> was opened on the M25 yesterday.	A new service station <u>offering more facilities to drivers than the older stations</u> was opened on the M25 yesterday.

Eine neue Raststätte, die Autofahrern mehr Serviceeinrichtungen bietet als die älteren Rasthäuser, wurde gestern an der M25 eröffnet.

Passivsätze werden mit dem **Partizip Perfekt** verkürzt.

long version	shortened version
The service station <u>which is run by a private catering firm</u> is open 24/7.	The service station <u>run by a private catering firm</u> is open 24/7.

Die Raststätte, die von einer privaten Cateringfirma betrieben wird, ist ununterbrochen geöffnet.

Adverbialsätze (meist Temporal- oder Kausalsätze) • Adverbial Clauses

Adverbiale Nebensätze können mit einer **Partizipialkonstruktion** verkürzt werden.

long version	shortened version
<u>As the Thompsons were tired</u> after the long drive, they went to bed early.	<u>Being tired</u> after the long drive, <u>the Thomsons</u> went to bed early.

Da die Thompsons nach der langen Fahrt sehr müde waren, gingen sie früh zu Bett.
[manchmal sind beide Übersetzungen möglich: **da – als**]

Wenn man einen **temporalen Adverbialsatz** verkürzt, muss man besonders auf das Zeitverhältnis (*time relation*) achten, in dem die Handlung des Gliedsatzes zu der des Hauptsatzes steht.

Will man ausdrücken, dass zwei Handlungen **gleichzeitig** verlaufen, wird das **Partizip Präsens** verwendet.

long version	shortened version
<u>While</u> Mr Thompson <u>was eating</u> his dinner, he thought about how to get to Dover quickly.	<u>Eating</u> his dinner, Mr Thompson thought about how to get to Dover quickly.
	oder *(mit einer Konjunktion + Partizip)*:
	<u>While eating</u> his dinner, Mr Thompson thought about how to get to Dover quickly.

Während Mr Thompson zu Abend aß, überlegte er, wie er am schnellsten nach Dover käme.

Will man ausdrücken, dass eine Handlung **zeitlich vor** einer zweiten liegt (d. h., dass sie vor der anderen abgeschlossen wurde), wird *having + Partizip Perfekt* verwendet.

long version	shortened version
<u>After</u> Mr Thompson <u>had eaten</u> his dinner, he thought about how to get to Dover quickly.	<u>Having eaten</u> his dinner, Mr Thompson thought about how to get to Dover quickly.
	oder *(mit einer Konjunktion + Partizip)*:
	<u>After eating</u> his dinner, Mr Thompson thought about how to get to Dover quickly.

Nachdem Mr Thompson zu Abend gegessen hatte, überlegte er, wie er am schnellsten nach Dover käme.

Beachte: In der deutschen Übersetzung steht im Gliedsatz das Substantiv, im Hauptsatz das Pronomen.	Having left the service station rather late, <u>the Thompsons</u> didn't catch the 5 o'clock ferry. *Da die Thompsons ziemlich spät von der Rast-stätte weggefahren waren, verpassten sie die Fähre um 5 Uhr.*

Hauptsätze

Im Englischen können zwei Hauptsätze mit einer Partizipialkonstruktion verbunden werden. Dabei steht die Handlung des zweiten Hauptsatzes in enger Verbindung zur Handlung des ersten Hauptsatzes oder ist deren Ergebnis.

Die Partizipialkonstruktion steht hinter dem ersten Hauptsatz und wird durch ein Komma abgetrennt.

long version	shortened version
Mr Thompson made sure their car was working properly. He <u>checked</u> all the lights.	<u>Mr Thompson made sure their car was working properly</u>, checking all the lights.

Mr Thompson versicherte sich, dass mit dem Auto alles in Ordnung war, und überprüfte alle Scheinwerfer. (= indem er ...)

Die zweite Handlung bildet einen Teil der ersten. In der deutschen Übersetzung wird daher ein eigener Hauptsatz verwendet.

3.2 Fehlerquelle: *Misrelated Participles*

Will man Sätze durch eine Partizipialkonstruktion verkürzen, muss man darauf achten, dass das Subjekt des Partizipialsatzes mit dem Subjekt des Hauptsatzes übereinstimmt.

Die Partizipialkonstruktion muss sich auf das Subjekt des Satzes beziehen.

long version	shortened version
When <u>James</u> arrived at the bus stop, <u>he</u> only saw the back of the 211-bus.	<u>Arriving</u> at the bus stop, <u>James</u> only saw the back of the 211-bus.

Als James an die Bushaltestelle kam, sah er den Bus 211 nur noch von hinten.

Aber: Im folgenden Beispielsatz stehen **zwei verschiedene Subjekte**.

long version	shortened version
	Eine **falsche** Satzverkürzung ergäbe:
When <u>James</u> arrived at the bus stop, <u>the 211-bus</u> had just gone.	~~Arriving at the bus stop, the 211-bus had just gone.~~

In der **nicht** korrekten Satzverkürzung ist nur noch ein Subjekt vorhanden: *the 211-bus.*
Das Subjekt *James* ist verloren gegangen. Die Partizipialkonstruktion *Arriving at the bus
stop* würde sich jetzt auf das alleinige Subjekt des Satzes, nämlich *the 211-bus,* beziehen –
und damit unsinnigerweise bedeuten, der Bus sei an der Haltestelle angekommen und
schon wieder weg gewesen. Es soll jedoch mitgeteilt werden, dass der Bus schon weg
war, als James zur Haltestelle kam. Wenn also zwei verschiedene Subjekte vorhanden
sind, muss man entweder beide nennen oder den Satz leicht umschreiben, indem ein
Verb der sinnlichen Wahrnehmung eingesetzt wird. Und das funktioniert so:

Um die Beziehung deutlich zu machen, kann ein **Verb der sinnlichen Wahrnehmung**
eingefügt werden: *to see, to notice, to realize* etc.

long version	shortened version
When James arrived at the bus stop, the 211-bus had just gone.	Arriving at the bus stop, James noticed (saw/ realized) that the 211-bus had just gone.

Liegen zwei verschiedene Subjekte vor, müssen beide benannt werden. Der Partizipialsatz
besitzt sein **eigenes Subjekt**.

long version	shortened version
As the petrol prices had gone up for the third time, the government had to think of a different way to increase tax revenue.	The petrol prices having gone up for the third time, the government had to think of a different way to increase tax revenue.

*Da die Benzinpreise schon zum dritten Mal gestiegen waren, musste sich die Regierung eine andere
Möglichkeit ausdenken, die Steuereinnahmen zu erhöhen.*

3.3 *with* + Partizip

Die Konstruktion *with* + Partizip wird sowohl im schriftlichen als auch im mündlichen
Englisch verwendet. Wichtig ist hier vor allem die richtige Übersetzung dieser Konstruktion ins Deutsche:

Beachte: *with* heißt hier **nicht** ‚mit‘!	He sat in his car <u>with</u> his hands <u>clutching</u> the wheel firmly. *Er saß in seinem Auto <u>und hielt</u> das Lenkrad fest umklammert.*
In der deutschen Übersetzung bildet man oft einen weiteren Hauptsatz oder einen Gliedsatz, eingeleitet z. B. durch **‚da, wenn, wobei, indem, während, als‘.**	I can't drive properly <u>with</u> you <u>telling</u> me what to do all the time. *Ich kann nicht richtig fahren, <u>wenn</u> du mir die ganze Zeit <u>sagst</u>, was ich tun soll.*

4 Übungen

36 Functions of the present participle (*ing*-form) – Explain the use of the *ing*-forms.

The triumph of nostalgia

The famous British motorbike producer Triumph went out of business, mainly because of the *rising*[1] tide of cheaper imports from Japan. After the collapse John Bloor, a Derbyshire millionaire in his late forties who started his career as a plasterer before *making*[2] his fortune in *housebuilding*[3], bought the rights to the Triumph name. Bloor was determined to get the company restarted.

A new factory was set up in Hinckley, Leicestershire and Bloor set out to develop a new motorbike model. He and his team even went to Japan to look for inspiration. After several years of research, The first engine was built in 1987.

To everybody's surprise, the new model has become extremely successful. With modern techniques the new company produces a bike which is as reliable as a Honda or BMW.

As a result, Bloor was able to increase the production capacity and expand. There was a *growing*[4] queue of customers *willing*[5] to spend thousands of pounds for a new Triumph. The new machines have succeeded in *creating*[6] a successful mix of nostalgia and technology, so a *waiting*[7] list still exists for the popular models. Says a Triumph dealer in Shepperton, "We are *finding*[8] that more and more people are *converting*[9] from Japanese motorcycles to Triumph. We can't believe it."

Today, Triumph Motorcycles Limited has factories all around the world. Apart from motorcycles, the company also designs clothing and is famous for *producing*[10] a big range of motorcycle accessories.

37 Using participle constructions – Shorten these sentences. Replace the relative and adverbial clauses by a different construction.

The world's longest cycle route

EuroVelo 12 *which runs* (_running_) from Norway to the Shetland Islands is one of the longest and most spectacular cycling routes in Northern Europe. As the route passes through eight different countries *which border* (_____)[1] the North Sea, cyclists can experience a large variety of coastal scenery. Those *who do* (_____)[2] the complete tour *which comprises* (_____)[3] 6,200 km in one go will cycle through Belgium, the Netherlands, Germany, Denmark, Sweden, Norway, England and Scotland. *Since cyclists will mostly pass through rural areas* (_____)[4], *they* must be prepared for varying conditions. However, those tourists who do not intend to cycle the whole route can easily find a section *that suits* (_____)[5] their needs and abilities best. The route *which was opened* (_____)[6] in 2001 was awarded a Guinness record certificate *which confirms* (_____)[7] that EuroVelo 12 is the world's longest cycle route. *As the route was planned* (_____)[8] along car-free roads, *it* can also be enjoyed by families and inexperienced bikers.

The British part of EuroVelo 12 starts at the port of Harwich and joins National Cycle Route 1 – a route *which runs* (_____)[9] from Dover in the south to the Shetland Islands in the far north. Bikers *who are interested* (_____)[10] in visiting historical towns and cities have easy access to places like Cambridge, York, Durham and Edinburgh, *which lie* (_____)[11] along the path. *When the authorities planned National Route 1, they saw to it* (_____)[12] that it was fully signposted in both directions. The most northerly section from Aberdeen to the Shetlands *which passes* (_____)[13] through wild mountains and along rugged coastlines is one of the most spectacular parts.

Cyclists *who wish* (_____)[14] to continue their route from John O'Groats to the northernmost point of the British Isles, on Shetland, can take a ferry *which connects* (_____)[15] mainland Scotland with both groups of Islands. *When you look* (_____)[16] *at* the number of bikers *who use* (_____)[17] EuroVelo 12 every year, you can easily understand the popularity of the world's longest cycle route.

38 Replacing participle constructions – Replace the participles in this text.

Holiday makers in Britain

Economic statistics *showing* (_which show_) the amount of money *spent* (_which was spent_) by people in Britain reveal that consumer spending is rising. *Feeling confident* (_____)[1] about their prospects for the coming years Britons bought more in shops and department stores. There is also good news for the tourist industry. A study by the British Tourist Authority *based* (_____)[2] on a random sample of adult British residents showed that the number of holiday makers *booking* (_____)[3] their holidays on the Internet was on the increase again. In addition, bookings *placed* (_____)[4] via mobiles reached new record heights. *Offering* (_____)[5] more bargain holidays than ever, local travel agencies managed to increase the number of holidays *sold* (_____ _____)[6] over the counter. The number of long holidays – i. e. holidays *lasting* (_____)[7] four days or more – *taken* (_____)[8] by Britons in the UK and abroad rose again, whereas long holidays *spent* (_____ _____)[9] in the UK decreased slightly. *Comparing* (_____ _____)[10] the costs of foreign holidays with UK holidays, many people decided to stay in the UK. And where did people *holidaying* (_____ _____)[11] at home go most? To the West country *comprising* (_____ _____)[12] Devon, Cornwall and Dorset. The new "suitcase champions" are the Chinese *spending* (_____)[13] more money on travel than Americans and Germans.

39 Time relation – Choose present participle or *having* + past participle.
Underline the correct form.

Examples:

> (<u>Reporting</u> / Having reported) on a recent study on night-time accidents, the chief police officer pointed out that young drivers were involved in more accidents than adults.
> **= gleichzeitig**

> (Driving / <u>Having driven</u>) for more than two hours, the lorry driver stopped at the transport café. **= vorzeitig**

Dangerous drivers on the roads in America

(Evaluating / Having evaluated)[1] the latest road safety statistics intensively, experts confirm that teen drivers are involved in more fatal crashes than adults. The worst time for accidents is Friday and Saturday nights. (Visiting / Having visited)[2] a disco with their friends and (having / having had)[3] a few drinks young motorists often feel over-confident. (Examining / Having examined)[4] the

reasons for unsafe driving, the police warn of the dangers of texting while driving. Many teens still send text messages (sitting / having sat)[5] behind the wheel. Inexperience is another reason for young people's accidents. (Allowing / Having allowed)[6] very young drivers on the roads many states have begun to review their policies. In Arkansas children of 14 may drive under supervision of an adult. (Driving / Having driven)[7] for two years teens can then apply for an official licence. (Causing / Having caused)[8] more serious accidents than any other group, young speeding motorists now face harsher sanctions. (Doing / having done)[9] more than 10 mph over the posted limit drivers are fined and lose part of their insurance cover in many states. (Announcing / Having announced)[10] a new campaign against speeding, the police are about to instal more red light cameras.

40 Correcting misrelated participles – Rewrite the wrong part in each sentence so that the participle is related to the subject of the sentence.

In London

0   * Getting up at 9, breakfast had already been served to my classmates.

    Getting up at 9, I realized that breakfast had already been served to my classmates.

1   * Being disorganized, ~~my London Transport Travelcard was left in the hotel~~.

_____

_____

2   * Walking on the edge of one of the fountains in Trafalgar Square, ~~my tourist map dropped into the water~~.

_____

_____

3   * After queuing for three hours at the Tower of London, ~~the Crown Jewels could be admired in their beauty and splendour~~.

_____

_____

4   * Standing on the battlement of the White Tower, ~~parts of the City of London can be seen~~.

_____

_____

5   * Returning from a visit to the Victoria and Albert Museum, ~~my suitcase had already been taken to Gatwick Airport~~.

_____

_____

6   * Looking out of the hotel window, ~~the 211-bus drove past~~.

_____

7   * Leaving the restaurant just after midnight, ~~a late-night bus was coming up the road~~.

_____

_____

* kennzeichnet einen grammatikalisch falschen Satz

41 Using *with*-constructions – Complete these sentences by putting in a participle clause introduced by "With …". Use the nouns and verbs given in brackets. Make sure you use the right kind of participle (present or past).

Sensible tourism

0   <u>With thousands of tourists pouring</u> into beautiful and unspoiled areas in the countryside, many conservationists are worried about the damage caused to the environment. (thousands of tourists – pour)

1   _____
tourism, more travel companies are offering tours for the "green" holiday-maker. (especially environmentalists – criticize)

2   _____
almost every month, many airlines are increasing their prices. (fuel costs – rise)

3   _____
from Gatwick Airport in the summer, the airport management have improved check-in facilities. (so many holiday-makers – fly)

4   _____ a new committee to look into the matter, there are now good chances for a programme called "soft tourism". (the Tourist Board – set up)

5   _____ to young people, the European community promotes mutual understanding between countries. (their many exchange programmes – offer)

6   _____ so much, many Britons are unable to afford a holiday abroad. (travel costs – go up)

7   _____ the entrance to the British Museum, none of the Japanese tourists could get in. (demonstrators – block)

8   _____ jobs in travel agencies, less staff is needed. (more and more computers – carry out)

42   Translating *with* + participle – Translate into German.

0   Sandra drove through the city centre **with** Harry **giving** her instructions now and again.
Sandra fuhr durch das Stadtzentrum und Harry gab ihr ab und zu Anweisungen.

William got more and more nervous **with** so many cars **following** close behind.
William wurde immer nervöser, weil so viele Autos dicht auffuhren.

1   Thousands of cars pass through the centre each day with filthy and poisonous fumes pouring from their exhausts.

_____

_____

2   With hundreds of noisy lorries passing through the city, shopkeepers in the centre fear that they will lose customers.

_____

_____

3   With petrol prices rising almost every day, more economical car engines must be developed.

_____

_____

4   Mary drove through the heavy rain, with the windscreen-wipers moving rapidly from left to right.

_____

_____

5   With more and more cars congesting our roads, the police have installed video cameras to observe the flow of traffic.

_____

_____

6   With so many young motorists drinking and driving, stricter controls are necessary, especially on Friday and Saturday night.

_____

_____

Das Passiv • The Passive

1   Form und Bildung

1.1   Einfache Form • Simple Passive

Die einfache Form des Passivs wird gebildet durch:
to be + past participle

On February 7, 1992 the Maastricht Treaty was signed by 12 heads of government of the European Community.
Am 7. Februar 1992 wurde der Vertrag von Maastricht von 12 Regierungschefs der Euro-päischen Gemeinschaft unterzeichnet.

Tense	Active	Passive
Present	Two new member countries sign the treaty.	The treaty is signed by two new member countries.
Past	Two new member countries signed the treaty yesterday.	The treaty was signed by two new member countries yesterday.
Present perfect	Two new member countries have signed the treaty already.	The treaty has already been signed by two new member countries.
Past perfect	Two new member countries had signed the treaty before.	The treaty had been signed by two new member countries before.
Will-future	Two new member countries will sign the treaty next month.	The treaty will be signed by two new member countries next month.
Future perfect	Two new member countries will have signed the treaty before long.	The treaty will have been signed by two new member countries before long.
Conditional	Two new member countries would sign the treaty …	The treaty would be signed by two new member countries …
Conditional perfect	Two new member countries would have signed the treaty …	The treaty would have been signed by two new member countries …

1.2 Verlaufsform • Passive Progressive

Die Verlaufsform des Passivs wird gebildet mit:
to be + being + past participle
Diese Form gibt es nur im *present* und im *past tense*.

At present the new EU regulations <u>are being discussed</u> in Parliament.

Tense	Active	Passive
Present	Channel 4 <u>is televising</u> the debate.	The debate <u>is being televised</u> by Channel 4.
Past	Channel 4 <u>was televising</u> the debate.	The debate <u>was being televised</u> by Channel 4.

2 Vertiefung

2.1 Verben mit direktem Objekt

Das **direkte Objekt** (= Akkusativobjekt) **des Aktivsatzes** wird zum **Subjekt des Passivsatzes**.

	Subject	Predicate	direct Object	Agent
Active	Six countries	formed	<u>the EEC</u>.	
Passive	<u>The EEC</u>	was formed		by six countries.

Einige Verben, die im Deutschen mit einem indirekten Objekt (= Dativobjekt) stehen können, werden im Englischen mit direktem Objekt (= Akkusativobjekt) gebraucht. Sie können dann ein sog. „persönliches Passiv" bilden. Im Deutschen gibt es dazu keine exakte Entsprechung.

	Subject	Predicate	direct Object	
Active	The P.M.	<u>advised</u>	the voters	to accept the treaty.

Der Premierminister riet den Wählern, den Vertrag zu billigen.

	Subject	Predicate	Agent	
Passive	The voters	<u>were advised</u>	by the P.M.	to accept the treaty.

Den Wählern wurde vom Premierminister geraten, den Vertrag zu billigen.

Folgende **Verben** werden im Englischen **mit direktem Objekt** gebraucht:

to advise = *raten*	to meet = *begegnen*
to approach = *sich nähern*	to obey = *gehorchen*
to believe = *glauben*	to order = *befehlen*
to follow = *folgen*	to remember = *sich erinnern*
to forgive = *vergeben*	to resist = *widerstehen*
to help = *helfen*	to thank = *danken*
to join = *beitreten*	to trust = *vertrauen*

2.2 Verben mit zwei Objekten (mit direktem und indirektem Objekt)

Bei Verben mit zwei Objekten (besonders bei Verben wie *to give, to hand, to offer, to send, to show*) kann **jedes dieser beiden Objekte zum Subjekt des Passivsatzes** werden. **Bevorzugt** wird eine Passivbildung mit dem **indirekten Personalobjekt** des Aktivsatzes (= Variante 1).

	Subject	Predicate	indirect Object	direct Object
Active	A new program	offers	young people	more jobs.

Ein neues Programm bietet jungen Menschen mehr Arbeitsplätze.

	Subject	Predicate	Object	Agent
Variante 1	Young people	are offered	more jobs	by a new program.
Variante 2	More jobs	are offered	to young people	by a new program.

2.3 Verben mit präpositionalem Objekt

Die feste Bindung zwischen **Verb und Präposition** bleibt auch im Passiv erhalten.

	Subject	Predicate	indirect Object	Agent
Active	The Cabinet	deals with	the treaty.	
Passive	The treaty	is dealt with		by the Cabinet.

Diese **Verben und Präpositionen** *(prepositional verbs)* bilden eine **Bedeutungseinheit:**

to agree on = *sich einig sein über*	to look at = *anschauen*
to agree to = *sich einigen auf*	to pay for = *zahlen für*
to ask for = *bitten um*	to rely on = *sich verlassen auf*
to complain of = *sich beklagen über*	to send for = *schicken nach*
to deal with = *behandeln*	to speak about/of = *sprechen von*
to dream of = *träumen von*	to speak to = *sprechen mit*
to hear about/of = *hören von*	to talk about/of = *sprechen von*
to laugh at = *lachen über*	to think about/of = *denken über*
to listen to = *zuhören*	to take care of = *sorgen für*
to look after = *sorgen für*	

2.4 Infinitiv Passiv nach Verben des Sagens

Die passivische Infinitivkonstruktion steht nach Verben wie *to acknowledge, to think, to consider, to know, to believe, to understand, to find, to claim, to report, to say.*

Active	Passive
People <u>believe</u> that the enlargement of the EU <u>will create</u> new jobs.	The enlargement of the EU <u>is believed</u> <u>to create</u> new jobs.

Man glaubt, dass die Erweiterung der EU neue Arbeitsplätze schaffen wird.

3   Übungen

43 Prepositional verbs – Put into passive voice.

From EEC to single market (1957–1993)

In 1957 France, West Germany, Italy and the Benelux trio signed the Treaty of Rome.

0   The original members of the EEC agreed on the abolition of trade tariffs.

 The abolition of trade tariffs <u>*was agreed on*</u> *by the original members of the EEC.*

1   In the sixties the six founder nations agreed to the removal of quotas between member countries.

_____

2   Even then many politicians complained about the slow-down in the further integration of the community.

_____

3 Pro-Europeans talked about a joint European foreign policy.

_____

4 Anti-Europeans laughed about the ambitious plans of a "European union".

_____

5 Delors and his collaborators in Brussels worked on the introduction of a truly free and open market.

_____

6 The EU commission can rely on the support from influential managers.

_____

7 Businessmen in Europe speak about the advantages of a competitive European community.

_____

44 Personal passive – Put into passive voice. Start your passive sentence with the underlined words.

0 Member nations must approach <u>the idea of a truly united Europe</u> in a determined way.
   The idea of a truly united Europe <u>*must be approached*</u>
   <u>*by member nations in a determined way.*</u>

1 Pro-Europeans will always remember <u>Robert Schuman</u> for his continuous work towards European integration.

_____

2 <u>In 1973</u>, the former EFTA members joined <u>the European community</u>.

_____

3 You shouldn't believe <u>critics of a greater EU</u>.

_____

4 Most politicians trust <u>the commission in Brussels</u> to find a fair compromise on controversial issues.

_____

5   Representatives of all parties met <u>the Queen</u> after her address to the European parliament in Strasbourg.

_____

_____

6   People ought to follow <u>the example</u> of the Danes who in their majority voted for an extension of the EU.

_____

_____

7   The knowledge of foreign languages will help <u>managers</u> to improve trading opportunities.

_____

_____

8   International companies have ordered <u>employees</u> to take part in a language training programme.

_____

_____

9   Businessmen advise <u>students</u> to learn at least three modern languages.

_____

45   Mixed tenses – Put into passive voice.

Foreign languages required

In order to achieve business success in a bigger European market foreign languages are vital. Yet Britons have been rather reluctant in learning them.

0   British managers and sales staff must learn more European languages.
    More European languages must be learnt by British managers and sales staff.

1   For years foreign language teachers have told British companies to train their employees in foreign language skills.

_____

_____

2   It is true that most schools in Britain teach French, but only one in three people can read a French menu.

_____

_____

3   Foreign language teachers regard the Britons' ability to speak and understand French as rather modest.

_____

_____

4   A large number of school leavers drop languages altogether at 14.

_____

5   Most Britons hold the view that they don't need foreign languages because everybody on the Continent speaks English anyway.

_____

_____

6   Recent research studies are showing a relationship between foreign language ability and export performance.

_____

_____

7   Not only managers but also secretaries, telephonists and receptionists need languages.

_____

_____

8   Especially small firms will have to do market research on the Continent.

_____

9   Companies with multilingual employees have achieved a considerable increase in sales.

_____

_____

46   Mixed tenses – Put into passive voice.

Towards a cleaner Europe

People in Europe hope that the new and enlarged EU will help to create a cleaner and healthier environment.

0   All Prime Ministers have agreed on the introduction of stricter standards of environmental protection.
    The introduction of stricter standards of environmental protection has been agreed on by all Prime Ministers.

1 The EU commission forces all countries to upgrade their environmental protection standards.

_____

_____

2 More British beaches meet community standards for water quality.

_____

3 Many cities are still pouring untreated sewage into lakes and rivers.

_____

4 All EU countries are introducing stricter limits on pollution from car exhausts.

_____

_____

5 Coal-fired power stations will have to reduce the pollution from their chimneys.

_____

_____

6 Planners have to take into consideration the effect a new motorway will have on the environment.

_____

_____

7 Before builders can lay the first brick, architects must study the impact of the new factory on humans, flora and fauna.

_____

_____

8 The EU encourages all countries to raise their environmental standards.

_____

_____

9 We expect all nations to contribute to a cleaner and healthier air in Europe.

_____

10 One hopes that the police will prosecute all trespassers of the new regulations.

_____

_____

47 Passive + infinitive – Rewrite these sentences using passive + infinitive forms. Do not mention the agent.

0   Economists believe the expansion of the EU is a success.

The expansion of the EU is believed to be a success.

1   People say that the enlargement of the European Union is a sensible move.

_____

2   Politicians believe that an extended EU will enhance (*erhöhen*) the security of all its members.

_____

_____

3   Critics acknowledge that the enlarged EU boosts economic growth.

_____

4   Politicians claim that the new EU provides a better quality of life for citizens throughout Europe.

_____

_____

5   Environmentalists expect that stricter EU policies will help create a cleaner environment.

_____

_____

6   Most people presume that the arrival of new members will enrich the EU's cultural diversity.

_____

_____

7   The general public thinks that customs controls are a waste of time.

_____

8   Everybody knows that air travel is less expensive than it used to be.

_____

9   They say that airlines are free to fly the routes they want.

_____

10 Economists report that restrictive practices between airlines are illegal.

_____

48 A mixed bag – Complete these sentences with the appropriate passive forms. Mind the tenses.

The Eurotunnel

There have always been plans to connect the British Isles with the Continent. Since the days of Napoleon plans to build a tunnel under the English Channel _____ [1] (draw up) and different projects _____ _____ [2] (develop). Between 1802 and 1985 as many as 38 different schemes _____ [3] (discuss) and _____ [4] (reject).

In 1987 a treaty _____ [5] (sign) by the French and the British government: a fixed link between England and France _____ _____ [6] (to be to/build). Of course, detailed technical plans _____ _____ [7] (not/lay down) in the agreement. The British Government, though, made it clear that the work _____ [8] (must/pay for) entirely with private money. So the race was on: the authorities _____ [9] (flood) with construction plans and suggestions how the link _____ [10] (to be to/finance). In the end, the competition _____ [11] (win) by a consortium called "Eurotunnel". The Eurotunnel engineers wanted twin rail tunnels and a service tunnel _____ [12] (dig) under the Channel between Calais and Folkestone.

Millions of pounds _____ [13] (raise) from international banks and private investors. It was obvious that financial returns _____ _____ [14] (can/only/expect) in the next century. So almost from the day it _____ [15] (give) approval to build the tunnel, the Eurotunnel consortium _____ [16] (trouble) by financial difficulties. More and more pounds _____ [17] (must/invest). The project itself _____ [18] (nickname) "Chunnel" – a word composed of "CHANNEL" and "TUNNEL".

Public fears and protests _____ [19] (must/overcome): Critics of the tunnel project pointed out that train passengers _____ _____ [20] (trap) in the tunnel in case of fire. Trains _____ _____ [21] (can/easily/attack) by terrorists and the passengers held hostages. The ferry companies argued that they _____ _____ [22] (drive) out of business, that thousands of jobs _____ _____ [23] (lose) in Channel ports. Environmentalists maintained that through the construction work the landscape _____ [24] (destroy). An almost endless number of meetings _____ [25]

(organize) by the Eurotunnel officials in which the general public _____
_____ 26 (inform) about all the details of the project. So eventually
construction work began. The tunnel _____ 27 (build) from
both sides – and in December 1992 the breakthrough _____
_____ 28 (achieve). British and French workers met almost 50 meters
under the seabed. At peak times more than 4,000 workers _____
_____ 29 (employ). Sadly enough, five British and two French tunnel
workers _____ 30 (kill) during construction. Safety precautions _____ 31 (question) and critics pointed out
that, on the whole, the French tunnel workers _____
_____ 32 (better/train) than the British.
So far critics of the tunnel _____ 33 (prove) wrong: jobs
are not lost, the damage to the landscape _____ 34
(keep) to a minimum, the ferries are still used by thousands of travellers.
After the construction of the tunnel one problem remained _____
_____ 35 (solve): a fast connection between the tunnel and London.
On the French side a high-speed line connecting Paris and Calais _____
_____ 36 (build). Until 2003, the distance from Folkestone to
London _____ 37 (must/cover) in trains running on
already existing slower lines. In September 2003, the high-speed Channel
Tunnel rail link _____ 38 (open). Since then the journey
time between London and Paris _____ 39 (reduce)
to as little as two hours and 15 minutes.

Präpositionen · Prepositions

1   Form

Präpositionen sind – in jeder Sprache – ein „weites Feld". Die deutsche Bezeichnung „Verhältniswörter" verdeutlicht, dass durch diese Wörter Beziehungen räumlicher, zeitlicher oder sonstiger Art ausgedrückt werden.

- **räumliches Verhältnis** zweier Objekte

  The book lies <u>on</u> the table.

- **zeitliches Verhältnis** zweier Handlungen

  My friend arrived <u>after</u> dinner.

Ein und dieselbe Präposition kann nicht nur eine räumliche Beziehung ausdrücken, sondern auch eine oder mehrere andere.

- Ortsangabe   <u>at</u> work

- Zeitangabe   <u>at</u> midnight

- Zustandsangabe   <u>at</u> rest

Die Schwierigkeiten, die Lernende mit Präpositionen haben, liegen in der Regel nicht im Bereich der Bildung, sondern vielmehr im Bereich der Verwendung. Übersetzt man z. B. das deutsche „über" in einem Text mit *about, over, above* oder *on top of*?
Angesichts der Fülle von Möglichkeiten, Besonderheiten und Ausnahmen sollen im Folgenden einige ausgesuchte Bereiche des Lerngebiets „Präpositionen" herausgestellt werden, die Sie sich am besten gleich insgesamt einprägen.

2   Gebrauch

Präpositionen zur Bezeichnung der Lage (*position*)

above = *über*	in front of = *vor*
before = *vor*	near = *in der Nähe von*
behind = *hinter*	next to = *neben*
below = *unter*	off = *von, weg*
beside = *neben*	on = *auf*
by = *(nahe) bei*	on top of = *auf*
from = *von*	under = *unter*
in = *in*	

Präpositionen zur Bezeichnung der Richtung (*direction*)

about = *herum*	over = *über*
across = *(quer) durch, über*	past = *vorbei*
along = *entlang*	through = *durch*
by = *vorbei*	to = *zu, an*
down = *hinunter*	under = *unter*
from = *von*	up = *hinauf*
into = *in, hinein*	upon = *auf*
out of = *aus, heraus*	

Präpositionen zur Bezeichnung der Beziehung (*relation*)

against = *gegen*
with = *mit*
without = *ohne*

3   Vertiefung

3.1 Hauptfehlerquellen

Präpositionen zur Bezeichnung der Reise und Bewegung (*travel and movement*)

to travel/go <u>by</u> bike/<u>by</u> car = <u>*mit*</u> *dem Fahrrad/Auto fahren*
to go <u>on</u> foot = <u>*zu*</u> *Fuß gehen*
to be <u>in</u> the streets = <u>*auf*</u> *der Straße sein*
to stop <u>at</u> = *halten* <u>*bei*</u>
to arrive <u>in</u>/<u>at</u> = *ankommen* <u>*in*</u>/<u>*an*</u>

Präpositionen zur Bezeichnung der Zeit und des Datums *(time and date)*

- **Uhrzeit**

  nach

  6.05 a.m.
  It's five <u>past</u> six in the morning.

  vor

  2.55 p.m.
  It's five <u>to</u> three in the afternoon.

  um

  8.30 p.m.
  I'll meet you tonight <u>at</u> half past eight.

- **Wochentage, Festtage, Monate, Jahreszeiten, Jahreszahlen**

  on

  <u>on</u> Monday
  <u>on</u> my birthday
  <u>on</u> Boxing Day
  <u>on</u> Christmas Eve
  <u>on</u> New Year's Eve,
  <u>on</u> the 13th of August

  at

  <u>at</u> Christmas
  <u>at</u> Easter
  <u>at</u> Whitsun

  in

  <u>in</u> August
  <u>in</u> the summer
  <u>in</u> 2014

Präpositionen nach bestimmten Ausdrücken *(after particular words or expressions)*

to agree with sb = *jdm. zustimmen*
to be angry with sb = *verärgert über jdn. sein*
to be anxious about = *besorgt sein über*
to arrive at = *ankommen in / an*
to be astonished at = *erstaunt sein über*
to believe in = *glauben an*
to depend on = *abhängen von*
to die of = *sterben an*
to divide into = *teilen in*
an example of = *ein Beispiel für*
to be good / clever at = *etwas gut können*

an explanation of / for = *eine Erklärung für*
to be independent of = *unabhängig sein von*
to insist on = *bestehen auf*
to be interested in = *interessiert sein an*
to be married to = *verheiratet sein mit*
a reason for = *ein Grund für*
to remind of = *erinnern an*
to be shocked at = *schockiert sein über*
to suffer from = *leiden an*
to be typical of = *typisch sein für*
to be white with (fear) = *weiß sein vor (Angst)*

[Beachten Sie in diesem Zusammenhang auch die *prepositional verbs* auf S. 86]

3.2 Typische Wendungen mit Präpositionen

• Wendungen, um nach dem Weg zu fragen	Could you please tell me the way to the museum? What's the nearest way to the museum? How do I get to the museum?
• Wendungen, um jemandem den Weg zu beschreiben	Keep straight on (,geradeaus'), past (,vorbei an') the traffic lights. When you come to the next zebra crossing, turn left into Bloomsbury Street. Go past the British Book Centre and take the second road on the right.
• Wendungen zur Textanalyse (writing about texts)	This is a report on (,über') the traffic problems in the capital. The text deals with (,handelt von, beschäftigt sich mit') the traffic problems in the capital. The text can be divided into (,in') three parts / sections. The author presents facts / information about pollution in the city centre. The writer comments on / gives examples of (,für') the housing policy of the city council. On the whole (,im Großen und Ganzen') / all in all (,alles in allem') I agree / disagree with what the writer says.

4   Übungen

49   Prepositions – A lesson in geography

Take a look at the map and then form sentences with the following words adding the proper prepositions.

0   London – River Thames → *London lies on the River Thames.*

1   Eurostar train service – operate – Brussels and London

_____

2   Isle of Man – lie – Irish Sea

_____

3   Ferries – sail – Liverpool to Dublin

_____

4 Bristol – reach – M4

5 Leeds – lie – Yorkshire

6 Blackpool – famous resort – sea

7 distance – London and Sheffield – 166 miles

8 Eurostar tunnel – English Channel

9 International companies – drill for oil – the coast of Scotland

10 London Eye – tower (verb!) – Houses of Parliament

50 Fill in appropriate prepositions.

London

London lies _____¹ the River Thames and is the oldest and largest city in Britain. Founded _____² about AD 50, it has more than 7.5 million inhabitants, speaking 134 languages. It covers an area of 1,580 square kilometres, divided _____³ 33 separate boroughs. It has been the capital of England since the Middle Ages, of Britain since 1709, and until recently was the centre _____⁴ the largest empire the world has ever seen.

London is an example _____⁵ how the size and splendour of a city may create problems and contribute _____⁶ its decline.

_____⁷ all over the world millions of tourists come to London every year to look _____⁸ its sights, thus adding to the already dense and often unbearable traffic in the city. Engineers and scientists have always been very good _____⁹ developing new ideas and technologies, but although wide arterial roads were built in the 19th and 20th centuries, the ring roads and fly-overs were unable to cope _____¹⁰ the thousands of buses, lorries and cars. For years Londoners had to put up _____¹¹ traffic jams and air pollution. Every day more than 2 million cars drove _____¹² the city _____¹³ an average speed of 17,16 kilometres per hour – in other words: millions of cars crept through the city daily! The traffic jams contributed _____¹⁴ air pollution because _____¹⁵ the toxic fumes emitted _____¹⁶ the exhausts of cars waiting at traffic lights. Environmentalists tried to make people aware _____¹⁷ the seriousness of the situation, warning that if nothing was done, Londoners would be confronted _____¹⁸ an environmental catastrophe.

Heavy traffic in the city centre was also bad _____¹⁹ business. Shopkeepers lost customers because congested streets and pavements kept shoppers away _____²⁰ the city centre. And as the prospects _____²¹ finding a parking place were bad – Londoners refrained _____²² a trip to the big department stores. Taxi drivers complained _____²³ the fact that their takings were down, simply because the traffic was so heavy and they couldn't drive _____²⁴ A _____²⁵ B in reasonable time.

A profound change came in February 2003, when the mayor of London came up _____²⁶ an extraordinary plan. Motorists in London were to pay £5 a day _____²⁷ the pleasure of driving _____²⁸ the centre of the capital _____²⁹ weekdays _____³⁰ six a.m. and six-thirty p.m. The new congestion charge aimed _____³¹ encouraging more people to use public transport, thereby reducing traffic and pollution in the city. It was obvious that a congestion charge could not be the final answer _____³² the traffic problems which have become so typical _____³³ big cities everywhere. However, it represented a first step _____³⁴ a solution. Mayors _____³⁵ big cities in Britain and _____³⁶ all over the world come to London to study the positive effect the congestion charge had _____³⁷ London's traffic.

51 Use these prepositions to complete the text.

around – at (2x) – between – in (6x) – on – up – with

The man who made air travel cheap

When he died _____¹ the age of 71 he was regarded as one of Ireland's greatest and also wealthiest entrepreneurs. He pioneered competition and low cost air travel, making travelling _____² Europe and the world cheaper for millions of businessmen and tourists. Tony Ryan was born _____³ 1936 in the County of Tipperary as the son of a train driver. He spent his early career _____⁴ the Irish airline Aer Lingus until 1975 when he started his own business. In a small office _____⁵ the Shannon Tax Free zone Ryan set _____⁶ an aircraft-leasing business called Guinness Peat Aviation. The company grew to become the largest airline leasing company _____⁷ the world, known as GPA.

In 1985 Tony Ryan launched a tiny airline, flying a small number of passengers internally in Ireland and _____⁸ Ireland and the UK. It made losses _____⁹ its early years until Ryan's personal assistant Michael O'Leary took over. Since then Ryanair has enjoyed tremendous success as one of Europe's biggest airlines. _____¹⁰ his death Tony Ryan left a family fortune of around £830m, making it the largest will ever to go to probate *(Testamentsbestätigung)* in Dublin. His will included property _____¹¹ Ireland, France, _____¹² the Spanish island of Ibiza and _____¹³ the United States.

52 Prepositions of place and time

Christina has booked a flight to visit her exchange partner Vanessa during the Christmas holidays in Belmont near Boston (USA). In an email Christina informs Vanessa's parents Ron and Geraldine about her flights. Write the email, using the information supplied by the travel agency.

From: Orbito Service <travelservice@orbito.com>   To: Christina E. Maier <ch_maier@...>

 **RBITO** AND GO! ™

Independent Travel WebSite
⇨ Learn more

BOOKING INFORMATION
Passenger(s): CHRISTINA ELLEN MAIER
Ticket type requested: electronic (e-ticket) Airline ticket number(s): 001197865845

Frankfurt – Boston, Friday, December 23
British Airways # 901
Frankfurt International (FRA) to London Heathrow (LHR)
Departure (FRA): December 23, 7:45 AM CET (morning)
Arrival (LHR): December 23, 8:35 AM GMT (morning)
Class: Economy

American Airlines # 109
London Heathrow (LHR) to Boston Logan International (BOS)
Departure (LHR): December 23, 10:30 AM GMT (morning)
Arrival (BOS): December 23, 12:50 PM EST (afternoon)
Class: Economy – **Seat assignment:** 41A

Boston – Frankfurt, Sunday, January 6
American Airlines # 2003
Boston Logan International (BOS) to Chicago O'Hare International (ORD)
Departure (BOS): January 6, 3:29 PM EST (afternoon)
Arrival (ORD): January 6, 5:26 PM CST (evening)
Class: Economy – **Seat assignment:** 27F

American Airlines # 84
Chicago O'Hare International (ORD) to Frankfurt International (FRA)
Departure (ORD): January 6, 7:30 PM CST (evening)
Arrival (FRA): January 7, 12:10 PM CEST (afternoon)
This is an overnight flight.
Class: Economy – **Seat assignment:** 38A

CHECK-IN INFORMATION
Because you're traveling with an e-ticket, no ticket will be mailed to you. Remember to bring a valid government-issued photo ID to the airport. All passengers are required to obtain a boarding pass before entering the security checkpoint.

53 Fill in appropriate prepositions.

A better past? Jorvik – lost Viking capital

A thousand years ago York was one of the largest, richest and most famous cities _____¹ Britain. A monk _____² that time described it as packed _____³ a huge population, rich merchandise and traders "from all parts". _____⁴ the 10th century people called it JORVIK, and knew it as the capital of the North of England, and one of Europe's greatest trading posts. It owed its prosperity _____⁵ the hard work and commercial enterprise of Viking settlers _____⁶ Scandinavia who had captured it _____⁷ AD 866 and almost totally rebuilt it.

Viking Jorvik has now completely disappeared. Most of the city's buildings were made _____⁸ wood, and have long since rotted away. _____⁹ some parts of modern York, however, near the rivers Ouse and Foss, which run _____¹⁰ the centre of the city, archaeologists have found remains of Jorvik. They are buried deep _____¹¹ the streets and buildings of the 20th century city. Here the damp soils have preserved whole streets of houses, shops, workshops and warehouses – even down to boots and shoes, pins and needles, plants and insects. Almost every aspect _____¹² life _____¹³ the time could be reconstructed.

York Archaeological Trust decided to build the Jorvik Viking Centre in the huge hole created by the excavations. _____¹⁴ the Centre people from the 21st century journey back in time _____¹⁵ the 10th century. The journey is done in time cars, which silently glide back _____¹⁶ the years, past some of the thirty generations of York's people, until time stops, _____¹⁷ a late October day in 948.

We see that the inhabitants of Jorvik look much the same as us, although they are not as healthy and far fewer than _____¹⁸ present will reach the age of 60. They are craftsmen making their products to sell _____¹⁹ the market. There they buy most of their foodstuffs, but they also produce some of their own. They live _____²⁰ cereals, field beans, peas, fruit and meat. Pigs are kept _____²¹ backyards and chickens run free in the city's alleyways. Fish is brought _____²² the city from the coast. Food is washed _____²³ with ale or as an occasional treat, with wine imported _____²⁴ Germany.

54 Fill in appropriate prepositions.

New York's historic landmark: The Empire State Building

New York is a diverse, growing city and the financial, cultural, and economic capital _____¹ the United States. _____² September 2001, this bustling and lively city suffered a terrible blow. The terrorist attacks _____³ the World Trade Center changed the city's familiar skyline forever. The WTC was opened _____⁴ 1973 and _____⁵ one year was the tallest building in the world. After the destruction of the twin towers in 2001 and until the opening of the One World Trade Center in 2014, the Empire State building became again New York's highest building. It is 381 metres high and has 102-storeys.

_____⁶ the 1930s Depression in the US, two of America's richest men entered _____⁷ a competition to see who could put _____⁸ the tallest building. One was the industrialist Walter Chrysler of the Chrysler car company. His architect William Van Alen designed and constructed the Chrysler Building, which was completed _____⁹ 1930 and rose _____¹⁰ 255 m. The other was John Jakob Raskob, a vice president of General Motors. He asked his architect William Lamb, "Bill, how high can you make it, so it won't fall down?" Lamb designed the Empire State Building, which gets its name _____¹¹ New York's nickname, the "Empire state". With its 381 meters the ESB surpassed Chrysler's skyscraper and became the then tallest building in the world. Construction of the ESB began _____¹² March 1930. Employing up to 4,000 men per day, the builders pressed on _____¹³ an enormous speed. Every day 60,000 tons of steel beams were delivered _____¹⁴ a rate that guaranteed that two stories could be completed. To save time, the building's posts, beams, 6,500 windows and window frames were made _____¹⁵ factories and assembled _____¹⁶ the site. Stones _____¹⁷ the skyscraper were cut _____¹⁸ the quarry. A team of 290 bricklayers was needed to mortar the more than 10 million bricks _____¹⁹ place. In November acrobatic ironworkers put the finishing touches to the tower that today houses radio and TV broadcast facilities. The Empire State Building was officially opened to the public _____²⁰ May 1, 1931. In 1986, the building was recognized as "National Historic Landmark".

Relativpronomen · Relative Pronouns

Ein Relativsatz bezieht sich auf eine im Hauptsatz genannte Person oder Sache und bestimmt oder beschreibt sie näher. Dabei wird zwischen **notwendigen/bestimmenden** und **nicht-notwendigen** Relativsätzen unterschieden [siehe Abschnitte 3.1 und 3.2].

Mit dem entsprechenden Relativpronomen (*who, which, that* etc.) werden Hauptsatz und Gliedsatz verbunden.	The popular paper <u>which</u> has sold most copies this month is "The Sun". *Das Massenblatt, das in diesem Monat die meisten Exemplare verkauft hat, ist „The Sun".*

- Das Relativpronomen für **Personen** ist *who*, für **Dinge** *which*.
- *that* wird nur in **notwendigen/bestimmenden Relativsätzen** verwendet.
- Auch im Relativsatz gilt die Wortstellung **Subjekt – Prädikat – Objekt**.

1   Form und Bildung

	Persons	Things
Nominative	who/that	which/that
Accusative	whom/who/that	which/that
Possessive (= dt. Genitiv)	whose	whose/of which

2   Gebrauch

2.1   Relativpronomen als Subjekt

Das Relativpronomen kann Subjekt eines Satzes sein: • für Personen wird *who* verwendet,	This is <u>the man who</u> has just been appointed editor of "The Bexleyheath Chronicle". *Dies ist der Mann, der gerade zum Chefredakteur von „The Bexleyheath Chronicle" ernannt wurde.*

- für Dinge *which*.

Letters to the Editor are <u>letters</u> <u>which</u> reflect the views of the readership.
Briefe an den Herausgeber sind Briefe, die die Meinung der Leserschaft widerspiegeln.

2.2 Relativpronomen als Objekt

Das Relativpronomen kann Objekt eines Satzes sein:

- für Personen wird **whom** gebraucht (besonders in nicht-notwendigen Relativsätzen; seltener *who*),

The <u>journalist Michael Billings</u>, <u>whom</u> we interviewed about his job, works for "The Guardian".
Der Journalist M. B., den wir über seine Arbeit interviewten, arbeitet für „The Guardian".

- für Sachen wird **which** gebraucht.

"The Guardian" is <u>one of the British</u> <u>quality papers</u> <u>which</u> our school subscribes to.
„The Guardian" ist eine der seriösen britischen Tageszeitungen, die unsere Schule abonniert hat.

3   Vertiefung

3.1 Notwendige oder bestimmende Relativsätze (*defining relative clauses*)

Notwendige Relativsätze bestimmen das Bezugswort näher und sind **zum** richtigen **Verständnis** des Satzes unbedingt **erforderlich**.
Der Relativsatz wird im Englischen **nicht durch Kommas** abgetrennt.

<u>Journalists who</u> write about the Royal Family have often been criticized heavily.
Diejenigen Journalisten [d. h. nicht alle Journalisten], die über die königliche Familie schreiben, sind oft schwer kritisiert worden.

A <u>paper which</u> publishes false information can be sued for libel.
Eine Zeitung, die falsche Informationen veröffentlicht, [also nur die, nicht jede!] kann wegen übler Nachrede belangt werden.

Contact clauses

- In notwendigen Relativsätzen kann das **Relativpronomen weggelassen** werden, wenn es **Objekt** ist. Relativsätze ohne Relativpronomen heißen *contact clauses*.

The papers (which) I bought yesterday have already been thrown into the dustbin.
Die Zeitungen, die ich gestern kaufte, sind schon im Mülleimer gelandet.

- Man kann das **Relativpronomen nicht weglassen**, wenn es **Subjekt** ist.

Where did you put the papers which were lying on the table?
Wo hast du die Zeitungen hingelegt, die auf dem Tisch lagen?

that als Relativpronomen

that wird nur in bestimmenden/notwendigen Relativsätzen verwendet.
Es wird gebraucht nach:

- *all, anything, everything, little, much, nothing, something*

Not everything that you read in the papers is true.

- Superlativen

"The Times" is one of the most influential papers that is printed in London.

- *the first, the last, the only*

"The Sunday Times" is not the only Sunday paper that offers a colour supplement.

3.2 Nicht-notwendige oder nicht-bestimmende Relativsätze (*non-defining relative clauses*)

- Nicht-notwendige Relativsätze sind **zum** richtigen **Verständnis** des Satzes **nicht** unbedingt **erforderlich**.

Alfred Harmsworth, who became Lord Northcliffe in 1905, published "The Daily Mail" in 1896.

- Sie bieten „nur" zusätzliche Informationen zum Bezugswort. Der englische Relativsatz wird durch **Kommas** abgetrennt.

"The Daily Mail", which sold for a halfpenny, was the first paper to carry advertisements to keep the price down.

- Nicht-notwendige Relativsätze werden meist nur noch im schriftlichen Englisch verwendet.

"The Independent", which is a successful quality paper, has recently re-launched its online edition.

- In der Umgangssprache bildet man meist zwei kurze Hauptsätze.

"The Independent" is a successful quality paper. It has recently re-launched its online edition.

In nicht-notwendigen Relativsätzen steht nach Zahlen- und Mengenangaben (*a number, one, both, many, most* etc.)

- in Bezug auf Personen: *of whom*,

  The journalists of "The Times", <u>many of whom</u> have been with the paper for years, are highly qualified for their work.

- in Bezug auf Sachen: *of which*.

  The British national papers, <u>most of which</u> are printed in London, are sold all over the country.

3.3 *what / which*

which wird gebraucht, wenn sich der Relativsatz auf den **gesamten Inhalt des vorhergehenden Satzes** bezieht.

The tabloids often publish exaggerated reports about the Royal Family, <u>which</u> annoys the Royals very much.

what wird gebraucht, wenn sich der Relativsatz auf den **gesamten Inhalt des folgenden Satzes** bezieht.

The tabloids often publish exaggerated reports about members of the Royal Family, and <u>what's even more annoying, about their children, too.</u>

4   Übungen

55   Match the definitions. Choose a sentence from Group B to complete the definitions of the terms in Group A, adding the appropriate pronoun.

Group A

0 [m] weekly = a paper *which is published once a week* _____

1 ☐ broadsheet = expression _____

2 ☐ colour supplement = free magazine _____

3 ☐ correspondent = journalist _____

4 ☐ editor-in-chief = journalist _____

5 ☐ gossip column = section in a newspaper _____

6 ☐ "heavy" = nickname _____

7 ☐ national newspaper = a newspaper _____

8 ☐ page-three-girl = young model _____

9 ☐ publishing house = a company _____

10 ☐ sponsor (of a TV programme) = a company _____

11 ☐ tabloid = a newspaper _____

12 ☐ tycoon = someone _____

Group B

a   caters for the taste of the masses (e. g. "The Sun")

b   covers "news" about the lives of famous people

c   finances a TV programme, e. g. a soap opera

d   is applied to the more serious newspapers (e. g. "The Times")

e   is in charge of the publication of a paper

f   is included in the normal Sunday paper, carrying lots of advertisements

g   is read all over the country (e. g. "The Guardian")

h   is used for the quality papers, referring to the size of the paper used for printing

i   owns several papers, radio and TV stations

j   picture is printed in a tabloid, mostly in a topless pose

k   produces newspapers, magazines and books

l   writes for one or more papers, mainly from abroad

m   ~~is published once a week~~

56   Relative pronouns – Fill in the appropriate relative pronoun.

The changing world of newspapers

In the golden days of journalism the British were a nation _____[1] read more newspapers than any other in the world. For many years the British papers, _____[2] readers came from all walks of life, sold millions of copies every day. And, _____[3] is just as remarkable, on Sundays circulations were even higher. So each Sunday morning you could see lots of people _____[4] went to the newsagents and came home heavily loaded with hundreds of pages of reading matter. Many Britons, some of _____[5] bought more than one paper, started their Sunday with a "good read", before they went out. However, these days are long over.

As early as 1980 London-based national papers, the majority of _____[6] had their offices in Fleet Street, _____[7] was also called "The Street of Ink", moved to Docklands, _____[8] is east of London, where modern buildings and more efficient printing plants were set up. _____⁹ publishers realized was the necessity to modernise production with computer typesetting. In order to keep production costs down, the most advanced technology _____¹⁰ was available at the time was introduced. Everybody _____¹¹ knew anything about the newspaper industry – and about competition among the dailies – was convinced that this was the only way _____¹² would guarantee survival.

In spite of all costly innovations, _____¹³ almost ruined some publishing houses, printed papers and magazines began losing readers to a dramatic extent _____¹⁴ nobody had foreseen. _____¹⁵ brought about the transformation of the world of news business was the arrival of the computer and the Internet _____¹⁶ happened in the 1990s. The feature _____¹⁷ threatened the existence of printed papers most, however, was the emergence of digital newspapers _____¹⁸ were available free of charge. The effects, the most important of _____¹⁹ were declining subscriptions and loss of advertising revenue, made some publishers close their papers.

Others, _____²⁰ spirit was still unbroken, published their papers online, but implemented a "paywall", _____²¹ means some online content was still free for users, but the rest had to be paid for. At first, opinions were divided: There were those _____²² saw potential in paywalls and sceptics _____²³ doubted the success of the system. To persuade their readers to pay for online content digital newspapers provided visual material (such as videos) and additional information _____²⁴ was not available elsewhere. _____²⁵ remains to be seen is whether the paywall system is the beginning a new golden era of journalism.

57 Defining and non-defining relative clauses – Decide which of these relative clauses are defining and which are non-defining. Put in commas where necessary.

Everything about TV soap operas

1 The early American soap operas on television which were developed in the sixties were daytime serials which were created to transport advertisements for housewives.
☐ defining   ☐ non-defining

2 The scripts which are written for the most successful BBC series "East Enders" have become more realistic.
☐ defining   ☐ non-defining

3 Most TV critics agree that the BBC soap "East Enders" is a drama series which – more or less – reflects society accurately.
☐ defining   ☐ non-defining

4 Today's American soaps show male characters who are often macho and tyrannical.
☐ defining   ☐ non-defining

5 A character to fit this description is J. R. who appeared in "Dallas".
☐ defining   ☐ non-defining

6 The new Director-General of the BBC who took over from his predecessor last week announced a change in the company's programme strategy.
☐ defining   ☐ non-defining

7 He said the BBC would remain a company which offers programmes for everybody.
☐ defining   ☐ non-defining

8 But the company would not follow the example of private broadcasters who try to attract a larger audience with ever "cheaper" – which means sillier – programmes.
☐ defining   ☐ non-defining

9 American or Australian soaps like "Neighbours" which brought fame to Kylie Minogue would no longer be shown on BBC.
☐ defining   ☐ non-defining

58 Connecting sentences – Combine these sentences, using relative pronouns and marking off non-restrictive relative clauses with commas.

A cartoon classic: The "Peanuts"

0 "Peanuts" used to be one of the most popular comic strips in the world. It was invented by Charles Schultz in 1950.

"Peanuts", which was invented by Charles Schultz in 1950, used to be one of the most popular comic strips in the world.

1 Charles Schultz's cartoon strip is still known all over the world. It has been translated into more than 60 languages.

2 The final name of the strip was "Peanuts". Its original title was "Li'l Folks".

3 In the early days newspaper readers didn't like the strips very much. Most readers were not used to the new kind of humour.

4 But the "Peanuts" became very popular. Their readership included people of every social standing.

5 During the 1960s a profitable merchandising industry was developed. It sold for example Charlie Brown clocks and Snoopy soft toys.

6 The strip's main character is Charlie Brown. Charlie has won the hearts of millions of readers.

7 Charlie represents the typical loser. He can never win the girl he loves.

8 A girl makes Charlie's life really miserable. Her name is Lucy.

9 Charlie is popular with only few members of the "Peanuts" gang. One of them is Peppermint Patty.

10 The death of Charles Schulz ended the run of the "Peanuts". Schulz' death occurred in 2000.

Zeiten • Tenses

1 Form und Bildung

1.1 Present tense

- **Simple form**
  3. Person Singular -s

  In Northern Ireland Protestants and Catholics <u>make</u> a new start.

- **Progressive form**
  am/are/is + -ing

  In Northern Ireland Protestants and Catholics <u>are</u> <u>making</u> a new start.

1.2 Future tense

- **Simple form**
  will + Infinitiv

  In Northern Ireland Protestants and Catholics <u>will</u> <u>make</u> a new start.

- **Progressive form**
  will be + -ing

  In Northern Ireland Protestants and Catholics <u>will be</u> <u>making</u> a new start.

1.3 Past tense

- **Simple form**
  Regelmäßige Bildung durch Anhängen von *-ed oder -d*.
  Unregelmäßige Bildung: siehe Liste der unregelmäßigen Verben!

  In Northern Ireland Protestants and Catholics <u>made</u> a new start.

- **Progressive form**
  were/was + -ing

  In Northern Ireland Protestants and Catholics <u>were</u> <u>making</u> a new start.

1.4 Present perfect

- **Simple form**
  have/has + past participle

  In Northern Ireland Protestants and Catholics <u>have</u> <u>made</u> a new start.

- **Progressive form**
  have/has been + -ing

  In Northern Ireland Protestants and Catholics <u>have been</u> <u>making</u> a new start.

1.5 Past perfect

- **Simple form**
  had + past participle

In Northern Ireland Protestants and Catholics had fought against each other before the British army arrived.

- **Progressive form**
  had been + -ing

In Northern Ireland Protestants and Catholics had been fighting against each other before the British army arrived.

2 Gebrauch

2.1 Present tense

Simple present

Simple present wird gebraucht, um auszudrücken, dass etwas **häufiger geschieht** oder **allgemein wahr ist**.
Signalwörter: *often, usually, generally, every Sunday* etc.

Religious differences divide the population in Ulster.
Religiöse Differenzen spalten die Bevölkerung in Nordirland.

Present progressive

Present progressive wird gebraucht,
- um auszudrücken, dass etwas **gerade vor sich geht** und **noch nicht abgeschlossen ist**.
  Signalwörter: *"Look, ...!", at present, at the moment* etc.

At present violence in Northern Ireland is decreasing.
Im Augenblick nimmt die Gewalt in Nordirland ab.

- Es kann in Verbindung mit einer Zeitangabe aber auch eine **zukünftige, festgelegte Handlung** bezeichnen.

Protestants and Catholics are meeting tomorrow to open a new youth centre.
Protestanten und Katholiken treffen sich morgen, um ein neues Jugendzentrum zu eröffnen.

Beachte: Besonderheiten der Schrei-
bung, wenn *-ing* an den Infinitiv ange-
hängt wird:

- stummes *-e* fällt weg,

  arriv<u>e</u> – arriv<u>ing</u>
  leav<u>e</u> – leav<u>ing</u>

- Endkonsonant wird verdoppelt,

  ru<u>n</u> – ru<u>nn</u>ing
  cu<u>t</u> – cu<u>tt</u>ing

- *-ie* wird zu *-y-*.

  d<u>ie</u> – d<u>y</u>ing
  l<u>ie</u> – l<u>y</u>ing

2.2 Future tense

Will-future

Will-future wird gebraucht, um auszudrücken, dass etwas **geschehen wird**.
[siehe S. 121, Abschnitt 3.6]
Signalwörter: *soon, in the year 2050,
in (the near) future, next week* etc.

The mayor <u>will open</u> another centre for
Protestant and Catholic youths <u>next spring</u>.
*Der Bürgermeister wird nächstes Frühjahr ein
weiteres Zentrum für protestantische und
katholische Jugendliche eröffnen.*

Future progressive

Future progressive wird gebraucht, um eine
Handlung zu bezeichnen, die zu einem
**Zeitpunkt in der Zukunft im Verlauf
ist**.

Parents from both communities <u>will be
working</u> together for a better mutual understanding.
*Eltern aus beiden Gemeinden werden zusammen-
arbeiten für ein besseres gegenseitiges Verständnis.*

2.3 Past tense

Simple past

Simple past wird benutzt, um auszudrücken, dass eine **Handlung abgeschlossen** ist.
Signalwörter: *in the past, yesterday,
two weeks ago, 2000 B.C., in 1912,
last month* etc.

During Easter Week <u>in 1916</u> militant Catholic
forces <u>rebelled</u> against British rule.
*In der Osterwoche 1916 erhoben sich militante
katholische Truppen gegen die britische Herr-
schaft.*

Beachte: Im Deutschen kann man hier sowohl Präteritum als auch Perfekt verwenden, im Englischen ist nur *simple past* möglich!
[siehe S. 119 f., Abschnitt 3.4]

In the 1970s Catholic and Protestant women in Northern Ireland <u>started</u> a movement for peace.
In den 1970er-Jahren <u>riefen</u> katholische und protestantische Frauen in Nordirland eine Friedensbewegung ins Leben.
oder
... <u>haben</u> katholische und protestantische Frauen in Nordirland eine Friedensbewegung ins Leben <u>gerufen</u>.

Past progressive

Das *past progressive* wird benutzt:
- um auszudrücken, dass etwas **während eines Zeitraums in der Vergangenheit vor sich ging**,

Even in Cromwell's days Protestants and Catholics <u>were fighting</u> against each other.
Selbst zu Cromwells Zeiten kämpften Protestanten und Katholiken gegeneinander.

- um die **Hintergrundhandlung** zu bezeichnen, d. h., es gibt zwei Handlungen in der Vergangenheit: eine von diesen beiden (sie dauert meist länger) ist die Hintergrundhandlung, die noch nicht abgeschlossen ist, wenn die andere einsetzt.
  Signalwörter: *while, when* etc.

<u>While</u> the demonstrators <u>were walking</u> down High Street, a car bomb <u>exploded</u> nearby.
Während die Demonstranten durch die High Street zogen, explodierte in der Nähe eine Autobombe.

2.4 Present perfect

Simple present perfect

Simple present perfect wird benutzt, um auszudrücken, dass eine **Handlung oder ein Zustand der Vergangenheit** einen **Bezug zur Gegenwart** hat.
[siehe S. 119 f., Abschnitt 3.4]
Signalwörter: *until now, (not) yet, already, ever, just now, since, for* etc.

The violence in Northern Ireland <u>has affected</u> the lives of Protestant and Catholic families.
Die Gewalt in Nordirland hat das Leben der protestantischen und der katholischen Familien beeinflusst.

Present perfect progressive

Während das einfache *present perfect* benutzt wird, um das Ergebnis einer Handlung auszudrücken, wird durch das *present perfect progressive* die **Dauer einer Handlung** betont.
Beachte: Im Deutschen Übersetzung mit **Präsens**

In Northern Ireland Protestants and Catholics <u>have been fighting</u> against each other for years.
In Nordirland <u>kämpfen</u> Protestanten und Katholiken schon seit Jahren gegeneinander.

2.5 Past perfect

Simple past perfect

Past perfect wird benutzt, um **zwei Handlungen**, die beide in der Vergangenheit liegen, in die **richtige Reihenfolge** zu bringen: Was zuerst passierte, wird im *past perfect* ausgedrückt, was folgte, im *simple past*.

In Northern Ireland Protestants and Catholics <u>had fought</u> against each other <u>before</u> the British army <u>arrived</u>.
In Nordirland hatten Protestanten und Katholiken gegeneinander gekämpft, bevor die britische Armee eintraf.

Past perfect progressive

Past perfect progressive wird benutzt, um die **Dauer der Handlung, die in der Vergangenheit schon vorbei war, zu betonen**.

In Northern Ireland Protestants and Catholics had already <u>been fighting</u> against each other before the British army arrived.
In Nordirland hatten Protestanten und Katholiken schon gegeneinander gekämpft, bevor die britische Armee eintraf.

3 Vertiefung

3.1 Einfache Form oder Verlaufsform?

Wie die Bezeichnung „Verlaufsform" bereits andeutet, ist die *progressive* oder *continuous form* eine Form und keine eigene Zeit.

> Wenn ein Sprecher die *progressive form* statt der *simple form* verwendet, möchte er vor allem die **Dauer einer Handlung betonen**.

Man kann von jeder Zeitstufe die *progressive/continuous form* bilden, z. B.:

Tense	Simple	Progressive
Present	Politicians <u>work</u> for an agreement.	Politicians <u>are working</u> for an agreement.
Past	Politicians <u>worked</u> for an agreement.	Politicians <u>were working</u> for an agreement.
Present perfect	Politicians <u>have worked</u> for an agreement.	Politicians <u>have been working</u> for an agreement.

3.2 Verben ohne Verlaufsform

Bestimmte Verben können **nur** in der *simple form* verwendet werden, **nicht in der** *progressive form*. Die Verben der folgenden Gruppen haben keine Verlaufsform:

Zustandsverben

to be = *sein*	to need = *brauchen*
to belong to = *gehören (zu)*	to own = *besitzen*
to consist of = *bestehen aus*	to seem = *scheinen*
to cost = *kosten*	to smell = *riechen*
to have = *besitzen*	to sound = *klingen*
to look = *aussehen*	to taste = *schmecken*
to mean = *bedeuten*	to weigh = *wiegen*

Verben der Wahrnehmung

to feel = *fühlen*	to see = *sehen (können)*
to hear = *hören*	to smell = *riechen (können)*
to notice = *bemerken*	to taste = *schmecken (können)*

Verben des Meinens, Wissens, Vermutens

to agree = *zustimmen*	to remember = *sich erinnern*
to believe = *glauben*	to see = *einsehen, verstehen*
to imagine = *sich vorstellen*	to suppose = *annehmen*
to know = *kennen, wissen*	to think = *glauben, meinen*
to realize = *merken*	to understand = *verstehen*
to recognize = *erkennen*	to wonder = *sich fragen*

Verben des Mögens, Nichtmögens, Wollens

to dislike = *nicht mögen*	to mind = *etw. haben gegen*
to hate = *hassen*	to prefer = *etw. lieber mögen*
to love = *sehr mögen*	to want = *wollen*
to like = *mögen*	

3.3 *always* + Verlaufsform

- Normalerweise deutet die Verwendung von *always* auf eine **Handlung** hin, **die stets abläuft**.
  Zum Ausdruck wiederkehrender Handlungen wird das *simple present* verwendet.

  Protestants <u>always</u> <u>celebrate</u> the anniversary of the Battle of the Boyne.

- Will ein Sprecher jedoch eine gewisse **Verärgerung über eine Handlung oder einen Zustand ausdrücken**, kann er *always + progressive form* verwenden.

  Both parties <u>are</u> <u>always</u> <u>complaining</u> that their rights are not protected.
  Beide Parteien beschweren sich dauernd, dass ihre Rechte nicht geschützt werden.

3.4 Simple Past – Present Perfect

Simple past

Im *simple past* werden Handlungen wiedergegeben, die in der **Vergangenheit begannen und in der Vergangenheit abgeschlossen** wurden. Das *simple past* ist die **typische Zeitform für Erzählungen und Berichte**.
Signalwörter: *yesterday, last week, last month, last year, in 1968* etc.

<u>In 1608</u> Scottish and English farmers <u>settled</u> in the richer parts of Ulster.
1608 besiedelten schottische und englische Bauern die fruchtbareren Landesteile von Ulster.

<u>In 1948</u> the Irish Free State (Eire) <u>became</u> a republic and <u>left</u> the Commonwealth.
1948 wurde der irische Freistaat zur Republik und trat aus dem Commonwealth aus.

Present perfect

Present perfect wird benutzt, um auszudrücken, dass eine **Handlung in der
Vergangenheit begonnen hat** und
einen **Bezug zur Gegenwart** besitzt.
Das bedeutet:

1. Der Sprecher möchte die **Wirkung
   bzw. das Ergebnis einer Handlung**
   betonen,
   - besonders wenn die **Handlung
     erst kurz vorher abgeschlossen**
     wurde,

We <u>have</u> just <u>been told</u> that a car bomb went
off in Douglas Street.
*Wir <u>erfahren</u> gerade, dass eine Autobombe
in der Douglas Street hochging.*
[Deutsche Übersetzung: Präsens!]

   - wenn **Dinge noch nicht
     geschehen sind,**
     Signalwörter: *not yet, never*

The opposing parties <u>haven't found</u> a solution
to the conflict <u>yet</u>.
*Die rivalisierenden Parteien haben (bisher) noch
keine Lösung des Konflikts gefunden.*

   - wenn **Fragesätze mit** *yet* **und** *ever*
     gebildet werden.

<u>Have</u> the negotiators <u>reached</u> a compromise
<u>yet</u>?
*Haben die Unterhändler schon einen Kompromiss
gefunden?*

2. Der Sprecher möchte ausdrücken,
   dass der **Zustand bis in die Gegenwart andauert.**
   Signalwörter: *since, for, all year long*
   etc.

<u>For years</u> the British government <u>has wanted</u>
to pass the responsibility for Ulster on to the
Northern Irish.
*Seit Jahren <u>will</u> die britische Regierung die Ver-
antwortung für Ulster den Iren in Nordirland
<u>übertragen</u>.*
[Deutsche Übersetzung: Präsens!]

Beachte: Hier kann sowohl die einfache Form als auch die Verlaufsform
verwendet werden:
   - einfache Form

Since 1998 rioting <u>has become</u> less frequent.
*Seit 1998 sind gewalttätige Auseinander-
setzungen seltener geworden.*

   - *progressive form* (um die Dauer
     zu betonen)

Since 1998 the British government <u>has been
withdrawing</u> troops from Ulster.
*Seit 1998 zieht die britische Regierung Truppen
aus Nordirland zurück.*

3.5 since – for

Sowohl „since" als auch „for" verwendet man mit der Zeitform *present perfect*. Es gibt allerdings einen Bedeutungsunterschied:

• *since* wird verwendet zur Bezeichnung eines **Zeitpunkts**, an dem eine Handlung begonnen hat.	The conflict in Northern Ireland has existed <u>since</u> the days of Oliver Cromwell. *Die Auseinandersetzung in Nordirland besteht seit Oliver Cromwells Zeiten.*
• *for* wird verwendet zur Bezeichnung eines **Zeitraums**, den eine Handlung bereits andauert.	The conflict in Northern Ireland has existed <u>for</u> over 400 years. *Die Auseinandersetzung in Nordirland besteht seit über 400 Jahren.*

3.6 Formen des Futurs

Es gibt verschiedene Möglichkeiten, eine zukünftige Handlung auszudrücken. Welche Form letztendlich gewählt wird, hängt davon ab, welche Absicht der Sprecher mit seiner Aussage verbindet.

• *will-future* Der Sprecher macht eine allgemeine **Voraussage** *(prediction)*.	We <u>will cooperate</u> with all people of good will to find a solution to the conflict. *Wir werden mit allen Menschen, die guten Willens sind, zusammenarbeiten, um eine Lösung des Konflikts zu finden.*
• *will-future progressive* Der Sprecher bezeichnet eine zu einem Zeitpunkt **in der Zukunft ablaufende Handlung**.	Both parties <u>will be talking</u> with each other to reach a compromise. *Beide Parteien werden miteinander reden, um zu einem Kompromiss zu gelangen.*
• *going-to-future* Der Sprecher drückt eine **Absicht** *(intention)* aus.	Make no mistake: we <u>are going to stand</u> firm by our principles. *Täuschen Sie sich nicht: Wir werden fest zu unseren Prinzipien stehen.*
• *simple present* Der Sprecher teilt einen **feststehenden Termin** *(definite event)* mit.	Talks between the parties <u>start</u> next Monday. *Gespräche zwischen den Parteien beginnen nächsten Montag.*
• *present progressive* Der Sprecher teilt eine **Vereinbarung** *(arrangement)* mit.	The negotiators of both groups <u>are meeting</u> in the P.M.'s office on Monday morning. *Die Verhandlungsführenden beider Gruppen treffen sich am Montagmorgen im Büro des Premierministers.*

4 Übungen

59 Mixed tenses – Put the verbs in brackets into the correct tense.

The Great Famine

Being an agricultural country, Ireland's crops and crop failures _____
_____¹ (always, play) an important part in the history of the island. The
country _____² (experience) its most dramatic years in the middle
of the nineteenth century.

After the Napoleonic wars in 1815, Britain _____³ (need) to import
more food. As a consequence of the increasing demand for food on the British
market, Ireland's agriculture _____⁴ (undergo) a revolutionary
change at that time. Up to the 18th century Ireland _____⁵ (be)
an importer of corn and it _____⁶ (then, turn) into an exporter of
grain and livestock. To meet the growing demand for food during the reign of
George III of England Irish farmers _____⁷ (seek) to increase their
productivity. They eventually _____⁸ (rely) on a root crop which
promised a high yield per acre: the potato. Potatoes were easy to grow and they
_____⁹ (can, serve) as a meal to people and they _____
_____¹⁰ (can, also, use) to feed pigs. The potato _____
_____¹¹ (emerge) as the staple diet of people both in Ireland and England
and _____¹² (bring) wealth to the country. Years of prosperity
followed, couples married earlier than before – which _____¹³
(lead) to a rapid population growth.

Disaster _____¹⁴ (strike) in the middle of the nineteenth century.
Between 1845 and 1850 one potato crop after the other failed, resulting in
widespread starvation and death. These years _____¹⁵ (know) as the
years of the Great Famine when millions starved or emigrated. The population
dropped by roughly two million. It is estimated that about one million people
perished from hunger and disease, the other million escaped from misery and
death by emigrating. The Irish _____¹⁶ (not, solve) the problem
of hunger and starvation by restructuring their agriculture. They emigrated in
large numbers, mostly to the USA, thus relieving the population pressure.

Even in our days that situation _____¹⁷ (not, change) a lot. From
1989 to 2011 the emigration figure _____¹⁸ (rise) from 44,000
to 60,000. Thousands more entered the US as tourists and stayed there, thus
adding to the already great number of undocumented immigrants. Illegal Irish
immigrants were unable to get a work permit, so they _____¹⁹ (must)
work as day labourers, cleaners etc.

Relief and new hope _____ [20] (come) in 1990: US Congress _____ _____ [21] (pass) a bill which allowed illegal immigrants to legalize their standing and to stay in the country. In recent years Irish Immigration centres _____ [22] (set up) in many US cities to provide advice, information, and support for Irish immigrants on issues related to immigration, employment, housing, career, education and social services.

60 Mixed tenses – Choose the right verb forms to fill the gaps.

> are – are looking back – arrived – became – chose – colonized – commemorate – declared – faces – give – has been – has existed – have always had – is condemned – represent – seem unable – was divided – wear

How Ireland was divided

For centuries the conflict in Northern Ireland _____ [1] a conflict between the newcomers and the former owners of the land. The tensions between Protestants and Catholics _____ [2] an economic background. In the 12th century the Normans under Henry II of England _____ [3] Ireland. The Protestants _____ [4] in Ireland, mainly from Scotland, sent by Oliver Cromwell following the setting up of plantations in the 16th and 17th centuries. That means that today we _____ [5] on 800 years of mistrust between Ireland and its former colonial masters.
The country _____ [6] in 1921 when the Protestants in the six northern counties _____ [7] to remain part of the United Kingdom of Great Britain and Northern Ireland. The southern part of the island _____ [8] a Free State in the same year and _____ [9] itself a republic in 1949. So the Irish Republic (Eire) _____ [10] for more than fifty years now.
The problem Ireland _____ [11] today is reconciling the two groups – the Catholics, which _____ [12] the majority on the island as a whole but the minority in the North, and the Protestants, of which the reverse is true. Historic fears and loyalties _____ [13] so strong that most people and even the political leaders of both sides – whether they are moderate or extreme – _____ [14] to move towards each other. To _____ [15] an example: Even today the Protestants _____ [16] the victory of King William III at the Battle of the Boyne in 1690. Indeed the Protestants still _____ [17] King William's colours (William of Orange from Holland – and the Catholics wear "the green"). It seems that each generation _____ _____ [18] to repeat the horrific and bloody disputes of the past.

61 Mixed tenses – Put the verbs in brackets into the correct tense.

From job famine to prosperity and back?

When Ireland _____¹ (join) the European Union in 1973, it _____ _____² (be) a poor agricultural country that _____³ (be) largely economically dependent on its powerful neighbour, the United Kingdom. It _____⁴ (have) a history of unemployment and mass emigration. In the 1980s one in five people in Ireland _____⁵ (be) out of work. The problem _____⁶ (be) at its worst in the impoverished West where those leaving to find work _____⁷ (reduce) the population by a third. There _____⁸ (be) many villages where the number of people between 20 and 35 _____⁹ (can, count) on the fingers of one hand. Virtually all the emigrants _____¹⁰ (be aged) between 17 and 30. Small rural communities that _____¹¹ (survive) the Great Famine in the 19th century _____¹² (be) unable to reproduce themselves because their maturing youth _____¹³ (go). The emigrants _____¹⁴ (be) usually the brightest and best qualified, who _____¹⁵ (can, find) work in Dublin, Britain or in Europe and America. They rarely _____¹⁶ (come) back. The situation _____¹⁷ (improve) a great deal when Ireland _____¹⁸ (join) the European Union in 1973. The country _____¹⁹ (benefit) financially from membership of the EU because it _____²⁰ (receive) a large share of the EU's Regional and Structural Funds. The money _____²¹ (invest) to improve the infrastructure which _____²² (facilitate) an overall improvement of the country's economy. Ireland _____²³ (experience) an unprecedented growth and _____²⁴ (often, refer to) as "Celtic Tiger".
Many Irish people who _____²⁵ (emigrate) in the 1980s _____²⁶ (come) back home. In 2001, the boom years _____²⁷ (end), and since then efforts _____²⁸ (make) to prevent a return to the days when Ireland _____²⁹ (nickname) "the poor man in Europe". However, the Irish membership of the European Union _____ _____³⁰ (also, bring) about social changes. The position of women in the workplace _____³¹ (improve) by passing the employment equality law. Other issues – moral matters related to the Church – _____³² (come) under revision. Progressive forces in the country _____³³ (fight) for more liberal laws concerning divorce, contraception, abortion and homosexuality to adapt the traditional views to more progressive European standards.

62 *For/since* + present perfect – Put in either *for* or *since* and use the verbs in brackets in present perfect tense (simple or progressive).

The end of the conflict?

Europeans have always found it difficult to understand that people living in a Christian country _____¹ (tear) each other apart _____² so many years. _____³ the days of the Plantation of Ulster aggression and hatred _____ _____⁴ (dominate) the lives of generations. _____⁵ the end of the "Troubles" relationships between the conflicting communities _____ _____⁶ (improve).

Talks about the economic ties between Ulster and the Republic _____ _____⁷ (intensify) _____⁸ the last couple of months. _____⁹ centuries the Northern Ireland economy _____¹⁰ (be) the smallest of the four economies of the United Kingdom. The traditional heavy industry such as shipbuilding, which dominated industrial activity _____¹¹ over a century, _____¹² (replace) by services. A museum dedicated to the Titanic, which was designed and built in Belfast, _____¹³ (attract) large numbers of visitors _____¹⁴ its opening in 2009. The myths and legends surrounding the Titanic _____¹⁵ (grow) _____¹⁶ the ship sank in 1912. In general, tourism in the province _____ _____¹⁷ (steadily, increase) _____¹⁸ several months running. With the economic upturn prospects for the younger generation _____ _____¹⁹ (never, look) better _____²⁰ end of the sectarian conflict.

63 Mixed tenses

A symbol of how much the relationship between the United Kingdom and Ireland has changed was the visit of Queen Elizabeth II to the Republic of Ireland in May 2011. It was the first state visit by a British monarch since Irish independence. King George V was the last reigning monarch to visit the country, in 1911, when what is now the Republic was then part of the UK. On the first day of her four-day tour the Queen placed a wreath in Dublin's Garden of Remembrance to honour the Irish rebels who lost their lives fighting for freedom from Britain.
The following is an excerpt from the speech which the Queen delivered in Dublin Castle.

Choose the right verb from the ones given in the box and put it into the correct tense to fill the gaps.

---

injure – stand – vote – painstakingly, loosen – experience – do (2x) – touch – now, come – always, not, be – imagine – set – also, shed – be (2x) – prevail

---

The Queen in Ireland

[…] Madam President, speaking here in Dublin Castle it is impossible to ignore the weight of history, as it was yesterday when you and I laid wreaths at the Garden of Remembrance.
Indeed, so much of this visit reminds us of the complexity of our history, its many layers and traditions, but also the importance of forbearance and conciliation. Of being able to bow to the past, but not be bound by it.
Of course, the relationship _____¹ straightforward; nor has the record over the centuries been entirely benign. It is a sad and regrettable reality that through history our islands _____² more than their fair share of heartache, turbulence and loss.
These events _____³ us all, many of us personally, and are a painful legacy. We can never forget those who have died or _____ _____⁴, and their families. To all those who have suffered as a consequence of our troubled past I extend my sincere thoughts and deep sympathy. With the benefit of historical hindsight we can all see things which we would wish _____⁵ differently or not at all. But it is also true that no-one who looked to the future over the past centuries _____ _____⁶ the strength of the bonds that are now in place between the governments and the people of our two nations, the spirit of partnership that we now enjoy, and the lasting rapport between us. No-one here this evening could doubt that heartfelt desire of our two nations.

Madam President, you _____ [7] a great deal to promote this understanding and reconciliation. You _____ [8] out to build bridges. And I have seen at first hand your success in bringing together different communities and traditions on this island. You _____ [9] new light on the sacrifice of those who served in the First World War. Even as we jointly opened the Messines Peace Park in 1998, it was difficult to look ahead to the time when you and I _____ [10] together at Islandbridge as we _____ [11] today.

That transformation is also evident in the establishment of a successful power-sharing executive in Northern Ireland. A knot of history that _____ [12] by the British and Irish Governments together with the strength, vision and determination of the political parties in Northern Ireland. What _____ [13] once only hopes for the future _____ [14] to pass; it is almost exactly 13 years since the overwhelming majority of people in Ireland and Northern Ireland _____ [15] in favour of the agreement signed on Good Friday 1998, paving the way for Northern Ireland to become the exciting and inspirational place that it is today. I applaud the work of all those involved in the peace process, and of all those who support and nurture peace, including members of the police, the Gardaí, and the other emergency services, and those who work in the communities, the churches and charitable bodies like Co-operation Ireland. Taken together, their work not only serves as a basis for reconciliation between our people and communities, but it gives hope to other peacemakers across the world that through sustained effort, peace can and _____ [16]. [...]

The Queen's speech at the Irish State Dinner, 18 May 2011. The Royal Household © Copyright 2010/11

64 Simple past or present perfect – Put the verbs in brackets into the correct tense.

The story of Guinness

Not everything in Ireland is gloom, depression and civil war. Most people when they hear the word "Irish" think of Irish folk music, Irish coffee, Irish stew. Irish whiskey (with an "e") is known all over the world – and so is Guinness, a special type of dark brown and bitter beer called stout.

It is more than two and a half centuries since the first barrels of Guinness _____ [1] (roll) down the slipway of a small brewery overlooking the River Liffey in Dublin. The face of the city _____ [2] (change) almost beyond recognition since then, and the small plant, which originally

_____ [3] (supply) purely local needs, _____ [4] (become) one of the biggest breweries in the world.

In 1759 Arthur Guinness _____ [5] (choose) four acres near the western entrance to the city as his site, the gateway called St. James' Gate. The name _____ [6] (remain), though the gate _____ [7] (long since, disappear). The brewery quickly _____ [8] (prosper). By 1782 – barely a decade after its establishment – Henry Grattan, one of Ireland's foremost parliamentarians, _____ [9] (declare) it to be "the nurse of the people, and entitled to every encouragement and exemption."

The Irish, never a race to keep a good thing to themselves, soon _____ [10] (spread) the word and as early as 1794 the London Gentleman's Magazine _____ [11] (carry) a picture of a Guinness drinker captioned "Health, Peace and Prosperity". By 1837 Guinness was well enough known to feature in one of the famous illustrations for the Pickwick Papers, but even before that, it was on record as having restored to strength an officer wounded at the Battle of Waterloo!

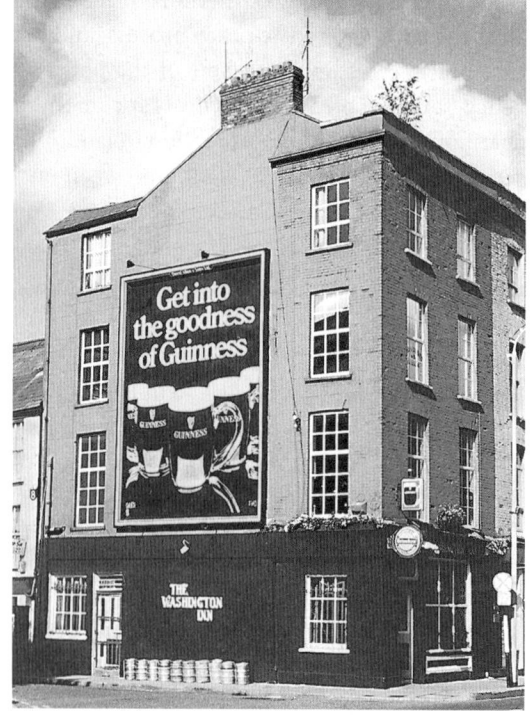

Today the brewery covers a vast complex, and for thousands of tourists a tour through it _____ _____ [12] (always, be) a fascinating journey through the centuries. On one hand you pass by picturesque old maltings and oaken vats, on the other a streamlined power house and enormous gleaming tanks. Since the firm _____ [13] (found) over 250 years ago, there _____ [14] (be) an unbroken family connection with it. All through the years there _____ [15] (be) a Guinness, a direct descendant of the founder, at the helm.

Tests

Test 1: Changing Places

1 Exchange visits can be fun or a traumatic experience all round. After I had celebrated my 13th birthday I played host to a 15-year-old French girl for a month. Her family vaguely knew a friend of my family. It was a disaster. Agnes, who lived in Versailles, came to rural south Devon and hated it.

5 Foreign exchanges are supposed to widen horizons, melt cultural barriers and, above all, improve children's ability to converse in a foreign language – or so the theory goes.

Every summer the tidal wave reaches its height with thousands of families up and down the country playing host to French, German and occasionally
10 Spanish schoolchildren. But is there really any lasting linguistic or social benefit from these annual experiments, which involve plucking young adolescents from their natural habitat and transplanting them to a land whose language and customs are totally unfamiliar to them?

What the people who provide you with Camille or Lukas for three weeks of
15 the summer holiday do not tell you is that, no matter how carefully "matched" the children have been, the outcome is dictated by luck. Parents are sometimes tempted into an exchange by the thought of being invited back to Provence and do not consider whether the teenagers will be compatible. But, if you are lucky, your children will go back to school speaking in a foreign language and
20 will also have made a new friend.

Philip, a 14-year-old pupil, was worried that he might not be able to understand when his French family spoke to him when he went to stay with them earlier this year. But he liked the sound of Guillaume.

"He said that he was interested in playing with computers and didn't like
25 sport, and as I hate all exercise which involves moving away from my computer, I suspected we might get on," Philip said.

In the event they enjoyed each other's company considerably. Philip's French improved as Guillaume was reluctant to try his English.

Guillaume was reassured to discover it does not rain every day in England,
30 and has taken to the rather relaxed British way of life. "I like eating toast at lunchtime and I'm extremely pleased about having everything on the same plate at dinner."

Worksheet: Changing Places

1 Put the sentence below into direct speech, starting: Guillaume said, "…"
Guillaume said that he was interested in playing with computers and didn't like sport.

2 Shorten these sentences using a participle construction.
   a) "*After I had celebrated* my 13th birthday I played host to a 15-year-old French girl for a month."
   b) "What the people *who provide you with Camille or Lukas* for three weeks of the summer holiday do not tell you is that the outcome is dictated by luck."

3 Put into active voice: "The outcome is dictated by luck."

4 Rewrite the sentence without using the words in italics.
"Foreign exchanges *are supposed to* widen horizons."

5 Explain the usage of the commas.
"Agnes, who lived in Versailles, came to rural Devon and hated it."

6 Rewrite using an if-clause.
"Agnes came from a big city. That's why she hated rural Devon."

7 Explain the usage of the *ing*-forms.
   a) "But is there really any *lasting* linguistic or social benefit from these annual experiments?"
   b) "Your children will go back to school *speaking* in a foreign language."
   c) "Guillaume said that he was interested in *playing* with computers and didn't like sport."
   d) "I like *eating* toast at lunchtime."

8 Put into passive voice: "Young children are using foreign languages."

9 Put into reported speech, starting: Guillaume said (that) …
"I like eating toast at lunchtime and I'm extremely pleased about having everything on the same plate at dinner."

Test 2: Homeless Teenagers

1 Government policies have produced a growing number of homeless teenagers and young people wandering the streets at risk from cold, hunger, crime, illness, drink and drug abuse, and prostitution, according to Shelter, the national organisation for the homeless.

5 Its description of the plight of the young homeless is illustrated by the publication of extracts from the diaries of more than 100 youngsters asked by Shelter and other advice agencies to describe a month of their lives.

The diaries reflect an existence dominated by lack of money, refusal of benefits by the Department of Social Security, efforts to stay warm and properly 10 fed, brushes with the police, and the search for shelter and work.

Shelter is calling on the Government to take immediate action to reverse the effects of recent housing and social security legislation. It makes 10 detailed recommendations to improve benefits and increase housing at affordable rents.

15 Mrs Helen Kay of Shelter yesterday welcomed a recent Government concession on 16- and 17-year-olds who can prove estrangement from their parents, but said much more needed to be done.

"To the vast majority of young people who contact us, this change won't make a scrap of difference because the extra benefit is only payable for 12 to 16 20 weeks," she said.

The report describes how recent legislation has reduced housing prospects for the young homeless and gradually deprives young people of state benefits in the effort to persuade them to stay with their parents longer.

It says many young people are forced to leave their parents' home because of 25 poverty, overcrowding, the breakdown in relationships and the need for independence.

"The real problem is not that young people leave their parents' homes, but that there is nowhere for them to go when they do."

"They face an endless round of moving from hostel to squat, from bed and 30 breakfast hotel to friend's home, and from one park to another, dependent on begging, charity and crime for support, and vulnerable to the dangers of drink, drug abuse and prostitution, unable to find work because they do not have a permanent home, and unable to find a home because they are unemployed."

Annotations
plight = *Notlage* / brushes = *hier: (kurze) Auseinandersetzungen* / estrangement = *Entfremdung* / to deprive of = *jdn. (einer Sache) berauben* / squat = *besetztes Haus*

Worksheet: Homeless Teenagers

1 Supply the appropriate prepositions.
While most Britons are aware _____ the housing problem _____ the capital London, there is a growing homelessness _____ younger people _____ the country. They sleep _____ the fields or camp _____ the beaches _____ the summer. One charity alone dealt _____ more than 200 homeless people _____ the last 18 months.

2 Replace by a different construction.
   a) "The diaries reflect an existence *dominated* by lack of money."
   b) "The plight of the young homeless is illustrated by the publication of extracts from the diaries of more than 100 youngsters *asked* by Shelter."

3 Put into active voice.
"The plight of the young homeless is illustrated by the publication of extracts from the diaries of more than 100 youngsters."

4 Put into passive voice.
   a) "Recent legislation has reduced housing prospects for the young homeless."
   b) "Shelter is calling on the Government to take immediate action."

5 Put into reported speech.
"To the vast majority of young people who contact us, this change won't make a scrap of difference because the extra benefit is only payable for 12 to 16 weeks," she said.

6 Explain the usage of the *ing*-forms.
   a) "Government policies have produced a *growing* number of homeless teenagers and young people *wandering* the streets."
   b) "Shelter is *calling* on the Government to take immediate action."
   c) "It says many young people are forced to leave their parents' home because of poverty, *overcrowding* ..."
   d) "They face an endless round of *moving* from hostel to squat, from bed and breakfast hotel to friend's home, and from one park to another, dependent on *begging*."

7 Put the verbs in brackets into the right tense.
Today in Britain more than 20 per cent of under-25s _____ (be) unemployed, and youth homelessness _____ (grow, steadily) at a faster rate than anywhere else in Europe. Shelter, the homeless charity,

_____ (estimate) that nationally there _____ (be) 150,000 homeless young people – and their number _____ (rise) in the future. Most youngsters _____ (leave) home after a row. Very often their families _____ (be) under financial pressure for some time, which _____ (add) to the domestic strain.

8 Combine these sentences with a relative pronoun.
The homeless charity Shelter estimates that nationally there are 150,000 homeless young people. 30,000 are in London.

9 Supply the missing relative pronouns if necessary.
Shelter has just published its annual report on homelessness, _____ is based on more than 100 diaries written by young homeless teenagers _____ were brave enough to tell _____ they call an "uncaring public" about their days of horror living on the streets. A copy of the report was presented to the Prime Minister _____ said that his government would try everything _____ was possible to relieve the teenagers' plight. But, _____ was even more important, said the PM, _____ wife and daughter were there on the occasion, was that whatever happened, teenagers should talk to someone _____ they could trust before they ran away from their difficulties – a reaction _____ would only make their situation worse.

10 Decide whether *ing*-forms or infinitives must be used. Supply the missing prepositions if necessary.
Parents don't want their children _____ (leave) home before they are in a position _____ (look) after themselves properly. But, more often than not, parents – too concerned with their own problems – stop _____ (talk) to their children about their worries. Mother is tired _____ (go) through what she regards as trivial discussions, Father might dream _____ (have) a quiet evening in front of the telly _____ (watch) football instead _____ (listen to) Little Zoe's school problems. Very soon, though, Zoe will give up _____ (turn) to her parents for help; she will see no point _____ (share) her anxieties with them any longer, and will one day think _____ (leave) home. If her parents do not bother – Zoe could well be in danger _____ (join) the crowd of homeless teenagers sleeping rough. If only people would try _____ (talk) to each other more often!

Test 3: Are You Eating the Right Kind of Food?

An Introduction to Nutrition

₁ The science of nutrition is concerned with the study of all processes of growth, maintenance and repair of the living body which depend on the digestion of food, and the study of that food.

A balanced diet contains adequate amounts of all the nutrients: carbohydrates, ₅ fats, proteins, minerals and vitamins. Hardly any food contains only one nutrient. Most are very complex mixtures. One hundred grams of potatoes, for example, contain about 18 g carbohydrates, 2 g proteins, 80 g water, and less than 50 milligrams of the minerals and vitamins.

The nutrient needs of adolescents are higher in many respects than those of ₁₀ any other group. Healthy adolescents have very big appetites. It is important that they should satisfy them with food of high nutritional value in the form of well-balanced meals rather than by too many high energy snacks.

Says one London nutritional expert: "Obesity among schoolchildren is now probably one of the commonest forms of malnutrition and this may continue ₁₅ into adult life. There is some evidence that adolescent obesity may be partly due to the general decrease of physical activity and hence in energy expenditure rather than to an excessive energy intake. A knowledge of nutrition and the incentive to apply this knowledge in practice is likely to benefit the health of young people for the rest of their lives. Dental decay is very common in ₂₀ British schoolchildren; sweet and sticky foods and snacks eaten between meals are one cause of this."

People who want to lose weight should cut down the energy intake to about 1,000 kilocalories each day. It is often convenient to cut out sugar and sugary foods such as sweets, preserves, soft drinks, biscuits and puddings as well as ₂₅ alcohol as these are mainly sources of energy rather than nutrients. Dieters eating three or four meals a day get better results than people who consume the same amount of food at one or two meals only; breakfast should be included. As it may take several months to reach the desired weight, a slimming diet should be sensible and palatable enough to be tolerated this length of ₃₀ time. Cranky diets based on one or two foods only are rarely successful as they are unrealistic, dull, and sometimes expensive; they can also be nutritionally dangerous.

Worksheet: Are You Eating the Right Kind of Food?

1 Fill in appropriate prepositions.
The foods eaten _____ other countries are very different _____ our own, yet the majority _____ people grow well and stay healthy provided that they get enough to eat. The reason _____ this, and the ways _____ which the adequacy _____ any diet can be assessed, form part _____ the science of nutrition.

2 Combine these pairs of sentences with a relative pronoun. Put in commas where necessary.
   a) "Carbohydrates provide the body with energy. They may be converted into body fat."
   b) "Fats provide energy in a more concentrated form than carbohydrates. They may also form body fat."
   c) "Vitamins are essential. Most of them help to regulate body processes."

3 Rewrite this sentence, avoiding constructions with *that* and using *for* instead.
"It is important *that* adolescents satisfy their appetites with well-balanced meals."

4 Put into reported speech, starting: The expert said …
"Obesity among schoolchildren is now probably one of the commonest forms of malnutrition and this may continue into adult life. There is some evidence that adolescent obesity may be partly due to the general decrease of physical activity."

5 Replace the participle constructions.
   a) "Sweet and sticky foods and snacks *eaten* between meals are one cause of dental decay."
   b) "Cranky diets *based* on one or two foods only are rarely successful."

6 Explain why no commas are used to mark off the relative clause.
"People *who want to lose weight* should cut down the energy intake to about 1,000 kilocalories each day."

7 Replace the word in italics by its adjective and rewrite.
"A knowledge of nutrition will *benefit* the health of young people for the rest of their lives."

8 Put into passive voice.
"Slimmers should cut down the energy intake to about 1,000 kilocalories each day."

9 Put into active voice.
"Breakfast should be included into any diet plan."

10 Explain the use of the *ing*-forms in these sentences.
   a) "Are You *Eating* the Right Kind of Food?"
   b) "Maintenance and repair of the *living* body depend on the digestion of food."
   c) "Dieters *eating* three or four meals a day get better results."
   d) "A *slimming* diet should be sensible and palatable."

11 Name the form in italics used in this sentence.
"A slimming diet should be sensible and palatable enough *to be tolerated* this length of time."

Unregelmäßige Verben • Irregular Verbs

Infinitive	Simple Past	Past Participle	Deutsch
be	was	been	sein
bear	bore	born(e)	(er)tragen, gebären
beat	beat	beaten	schlagen
begin	began	begun	beginnen
bet	bet	bet	wetten
bind	bound	bound	binden
bite	bit	bit(ten)	beißen
bleed	bled	bled	bluten
blow	blew	blown	blasen
break	broke	broken	brechen
bring	brought	brought	bringen
build	built	built	bauen
burn	burnt/burned	burnt/burned	brennen
burst	burst	burst	platzen
buy	bought	bought	kaufen
catch	caught	caught	fangen
choose	chose	chosen	wählen
come	came	come	kommen
cost	cost	cost	kosten
cut	cut	cut	schneiden
deal	dealt	dealt	handeln
dig	dug	dug	graben
do	did	done	tun
draw	drew	drawn	zeichnen, ziehen
dream	dreamt/dreamed	dreamt/dreamed	träumen

Infinitive	Simple Past	Past Participle	Deutsch
drink	drank	drunk	trinken
drive	drove	driven	fahren
eat	ate	eaten	essen
fall	fell	fallen	fallen
feed	fed	fed	füttern
feel	felt	felt	fühlen
fight	fought	fought	kämpfen
find	found	found	finden
flee	fled	fled	fliehen
fly	flew	flown	fliegen
forbid	forbade	forbidden	verbieten
forget	forgot	forgotten	vergessen
forgive	forgave	forgiven	vergeben
freeze	froze	frozen	frieren
get	got	got	bekommen
give	gave	given	geben
go	went	gone	gehen
grow	grew	grown	wachsen
hang	hung	hung	hängen
have	had	had	haben
hear	heard	heard	hören
hide	hid	hidden	verstecken
hit	hit	hit	treffen, schlagen
hold	held	held	halten
hurt	hurt	hurt	verletzen
keep	kept	kept	halten
know	knew	known	wissen
lay	laid	laid	legen
lead	led	led	leiten
lean	leant/leaned	leant/leaned	lehnen
learn	learnt/learned	learnt/learned	lernen

Infinitive	Simple Past	Past Participle	Deutsch
leave	left	left	lassen
lend	lent	lent	leihen
let	let	let	lassen
lie	lay	lain	liegen
light	lit/lighted	lit/lighted	beleuchten
lose	lost	lost	verlieren
make	made	made	machen
mean	meant	meant	meinen, bedeuten
meet	met	met	treffen
pay	paid	paid	bezahlen
put	put	put	setzen, stellen, legen
read	read	read	lesen
ride	rode	ridden	fahren, reiten
ring	rang	rung	läuten
rise	rose	risen	aufstehen, aufgehen
run	ran	run	laufen, rennen
say	said	said	sagen
see	saw	seen	sehen
seek	sought	sought	suchen
sell	sold	sold	verkaufen
send	sent	sent	senden
set	set	set	setzen, stellen
sew	sewed	sown	nähen
shake	shook	shaken	schütteln
shine	shone	shone	scheinen
shoot	shot	shot	schießen
show	showed	shown	zeigen
shrink	shrank	shrunk	schrumpfen, einlaufen
shut	shut	shut	schließen
sing	sang	sung	singen
sink	sank	sunk	sinken

Infinitive	Simple Past	Past Participle	Deutsch
sit	sat	sat	sitzen
sleep	slept	slept	schlafen
smell	smelt	smelt	riechen
speak	spoke	spoken	sprechen
spell	spelt	spelt	buchstabieren
spend	spent	spent	verbringen, ausgeben
spill	spilt/spilled	spilt/spilled	verschütten
split	split	split	spalten, teilen
spoil	spoilt/spoiled	spoilt/spoiled	verderben
spread	spread	spread	ausbreiten
spring	sprang	sprung	springen
stand	stood	stood	stehen
steal	stole	stolen	stehlen
stick	stuck	stuck	kleben
strike	struck	struck	stoßen, schlagen
swear	swore	sworn	fluchen, schwören
sweep	swept	swept	fegen
swim	swam	swum	schwimmen
swing	swung	swung	schwingen
take	took	taken	nehmen
teach	taught	taught	lehren
tear	tore	torn	reißen
tell	told	told	erzählen
think	thought	thought	denken, glauben
throw	threw	thrown	werfen
understand	understood	understood	verstehen
wake	woke	woken	aufwachen, wecken
wear	wore	worn	tragen
win	won	won	gewinnen
write	wrote	written	schreiben

Lösungen · Key

Das Adverb • The Adverb

1 1 legally / 2 heavily/ 3 regularly / 4 hard / 5 eventually / 6 carefully /
7 gradually / 8 finally / 9 easy / 10 comfortable / 11 happy / 12 openly /
13 tremendously / 14 violently / 15 close / 16 total / 17 good

2 1 greatly contributed / 2 hardly surprising / 3 generally accepted /
4 fairly easy / 5 completely different / 6 especially dramatic / 7 unusually low/
8 fairly static / 9 seriously injured / 10 comparatively strict /
11 initially criticized / 12 absolutely unfair

3 1 insignficant / 2 arguably / 3 unknown / 4 emotionally / 5 physically /
6 confidential / 7 helpless / 8 usually / 9 Consequently / 10 largely /
11 merely / 12 dramatically / 13 quickly / 14 special / 15 specially /
16 comfortable / 17 explicitly / 18 separately / 19 surprisingly /
20 continuous / 21 negative / 22 accidentally

4 a) 1 eventually / 2 finally / 3 initially / 4 largely / 5 recreational /
6 especially / 7 astonishing / 8 sole
  b) 1 negative / 2 potentially / 3 frequently / 4 addictive / 5 regular /
6 physiological / 7 clear / 8 severely / 9 unpredictable / 10 free /
11 unarguable / 12 admirable

5 1 This leaflet explains what happens at a criminal trial and your part in it.
  2 On your first morning at court a member of the court staff will tell you
more about the duties of jurors.
  3 Jury service normally lasts for ten working days.
  4 If a trial is likely to last longer, you will be asked if this would cause any
difficulty.
  5 There is no fairer way of deciding facts than to take twelve people selected
at random.
  6 Their job is to listen carefully to all that takes place during the trial.
  7 Then they go to the juryroom and pool their experience, common sense
and wisdom to reach a proper verdict.

8 It is most important that you do not discuss the case with anybody except other members of your jury.
9 Any discussion should take place in the privacy of the jury room when all the jurors are present.
10 It is an offence for any person to try to influence you in any way.
11 If anyone speaks to you about the case, you should report the matter immediately to the court or any police officer.

Der Artikel • The Article

6 1 a / 2 the / 3 a / 4 the / 5 the / 6 a / 7 a / 8 The / 9 the / 10 the / 11 – / 12 a / 13 the / 14 the / 15 – / 16 a / 17 – / 18 – / 19 the / 20 –

7 1 – / 2 – / 3 – / 4 a / 5 a / 6 – / 7 a / 8 a / 9 – / 10 the / 11 an / 12 an / 13 a / 14 a / 15 a / 16 – / 17 the / 18 the / 19 the / 20 a / 21 a / 22 – / 23 a / 24 the / 25 – / 26 a / 27 the / 28 – / 29 –

8 1 the / 2 an / 3 the / 4 an / 5 a / 6 the / 7 a / 8 the / 9 an / 10 the / 11 a / 12 a / 13 a / 14 the / 15 the / 16 a / 17 the / 18 the / 19 the / 20 the / 21 a / 22 the

Bedingungssätze • Conditional Sentences

9 1 will have to cooperate / 2 are to stop / 3 won't be able to save / 4 won't be solved / 5 will have to consider / 6 won't be / 7 will have to convince / 8 won't be able to conserve / 9 will be / 10 will be

10 1 would be able to, could cope / 2 would be / 3 had to pay / 4 were / 5 drove / 6 were / 7 might be saved / 8 received / 9 would be

11 1 If more packages **were** environment-friendly, it **wouldn't be** so difficult and expensive to dispose of them properly.
2 If so many wrappings **weren't needed** due to hygiene requirements, we **wouldn't have to keep** them.
3 If some people **weren't** still **used** to throwing everything into one bin, it **wouldn't be** impossible (it **would be** possible) to burn all the rubbish.
4 If all people **sorted** their household waste, it **wouldn't have to be done** in special recycling plants.

5 If plastic containers **weren't** still so cheap, they **wouldn't be used** a lot.
6 If many people **weren't** too lazy to take their empty bottles to the bottle bank, their dustbins **wouldn't be** so full.
7 If more smokers **were** environmentally conscious, they **wouldn't throw** their cigarette ends all over the place.
8 If yellow sacks **weren't distributed** free of charge, irresponsible people **wouldn't use** them instead of dustbins.

12 1 If the ship's hull **hadn't been cracked**, none of the oil **would have leaked** / the oil **wouldn't have leaked**.
2 If the ship **hadn't been** so close to the shore, fewer animals **would have been killed** by spilled oil.
3 If the oil **hadn't reached** popular surfing spots, MARITIME NEW ZEALAND **wouldn't have had to close** any of the beaches along the coast to the public.
4 If thousands of volunteers **hadn't helped to clean** the beaches, many seabirds **wouldn't have survived** / fewer seabirds **would have survived**.
5 If there **hadn't been** strong winds, none of the containers **would have been washed** overboard.
6 If the containers **hadn't carried** / If none of the containers **had carried** hazardous materials, the authorities **wouldn't have worried** that contact with water could lead to dangerous chemical reactions.
7 If the weather conditions off the coast **hadn't been** so rough, the salvage team **wouldn't have had to wait** with their rescue operation.
8 If the weather **hadn't calmed** down at last, the salvage experts **couldn't have pumped** the remaining oil to a barge.

13 1 If I didn't have a separate room for storing things, I would not put them in the hall or corridor.
2 If I didn't have a fixed heating system, I would use a convector heater.
3 If a fire broke out in my room, I would leave the room immediately.
4 If there were other people in the house, I would inform them and make them leave the building.
5 If the normal escape routes were blocked, I would use the balcony.
6 If a fire broke out in another part of the building, I would stay in my home and call the fire brigade.
7 If smoke came into my flat, I would leave it at once.
8 I would only evacuate the building if the Fire Brigade told me so.

Das Gerundium • The Gerund

14 1 worth(while) reading / 2 give up, stop treating Shakespeare ... / 3 were sick of spending ... / 4 were tired of going / 5 we would not have any difficulty in writing / 6 enjoy performing / 7 we are interested in, enjoy acting / 8 we had difficulty in choosing / 9 we couldn't dream of performing that play / 10 of members of our group feeling / 11 How about staging / 12 succeeded in picking / 13 looking forward to spending / 14 cannot, can't stop worrying / 15 There's no (way of) telling / 16 There's no denying / 17 be worthwhile trying

15 1 insisted on going / 2 wanted to prevent his class from losing / 3 prevent Macbeth from committing / 4 is clever at acting. / 5 has difficulty in learning / 6 liked the idea of telling / 7 succeeded in getting / 8 insists on young actors taking

16 1 going / 2 visiting / 3 coming / 4 visiting / 5 to find / 6 being / 7 to say / 8 packing / 9 leaving / 10 to try / 11 to find / 12 to squeeze / 13 driving / 14 looking / 15 in finding / 16 queuing / 17 to get / 18 trying / 19 seeing / 20 to get / 21 listening / 22 coming / 23 coming / 24 to enjoy

17 1 working / 2 Emily working / 3 (their) not being able to go / 4 has hopes of getting / 5 (their) having to sit / 6 Emily complaining / 7 for having to return / 8 me, my not buying / 9 their dressing up / 10 on Jacob not turning up

Modale Hilfsverben • Modal Auxiliaries

18
1 ... Jenny **will be able to look** after her baby.
2 ... Jenny **has been able to look** after her baby.
3 ... Jenny **will be able to look** after her baby.
4 ... Jenny **would be able to/could look** after her baby.
5 ... Jenny **has been able to look** after her baby.
6 ... Jenny and her husband **had to cope** with less money.
7 ... Jenny and her husband **have had to cope** with less money.
8 ... Jenny and her husband **will have to cope** with less money.
9 ... Jenny and her husband **will have to cope** with less money.
10 ... Jenny and her husband **wouldn't have to cope** with less money.

19 1 Jenny and Terry **haven't had to change** a lot since the baby was born.
2 Jenny **doesn't have to/needn't get** her baby daughter to bed before seven.
3 She **doesn't have to/needn't wash** up all the baby bottles.
4 Last week she **didn't have to change** the baby's nappies seven times a day.
5 When Jenny and Terry get a baby-sitter they **won't have to pay** her in advance.
6 When the baby cries Jenny **doesn't have to/needn't answer** at once.
7 Next week Jenny and Terry **won't have to buy** a new baby pram.

20 1 … I **won't have to cope** with my full-time job and bring up my children at the same time.
2 … I **wouldn't have to cope** with my full-time job and bring up my children at the same time.
3 … managers **won't be able to afford to lose** qualified female staff.
4 … managers **couldn't afford to lose** qualified female staff.
5 … managers **haven't been able to afford to lose** qualified female staff.
6 … managers **cannot afford to lose** qualified female staff.

21 1 ought to, should be / 2 shouldn't be / 3 ought not to, shouldn't be seen / 4 ought to, should do / 5 should, ought to be / 6 are we to solve / 7 Shall we send / 8 should / 9 is the city to provide / 10 is to be built / 11 should make / 12 ought to, should help

22 1 May I turn your attention to a topical problem: the employment of illegal immigrants as domestic helpers.
2 It is said that even prominent US politicians (Even prominent US politicians are said to) have employed illegal immigrants as nannies for example.
3 Of course, foreigners may be employed as domestic helpers; by the way you mustn't call them "servants".
4 The employer must make sure that he only gives work to foreigners who have a work permit.
5 So before you employ someone you should / ought to ask for documentation.
6 Of course, social security is to be paid.
7 In recent years American couples simply couldn't find a nanny on the job market.
8 Therefore they were extremely pleased when they could finally employ an immigrant.

9 Besides labour was cheap: of course, illegal workers cannot expect the same wages as legal workers.
10 More than one politician could have stayed in office if he had not employed an illegal home help.

Indirekte Rede • Reported Speech

23 At the press conference the manager of BIG BURGER **said** food hygiene and quality **had always been** important to **his** company. He **told** the journalists that there **had been** much debate recently regarding the quality of meat used in the fast service restaurant industry. Holstein **assured us** that only prime cuts of lean forequarter and flank **were used** for **their** 100 % pure beef hamburgers. **They used** no additives; no fillers, no binders, no flavour enhancers. The manager **stressed the fact** that **their** beef **came** from EU approved European suppliers. Every consignment of beef **was** subject to a total of 36 quality control checks. He **added** that if a consignment **should fail** on any one check – it **would be rejected** by BIG BURGER. In addition, a Ministry of Agriculture representative **visited** the plant weekly to monitor its hygiene standards.
Holstein **went on** that BIG BURGER **had** always **been** very conscious of all issues relating to the environment, including unnecessary outer packaging. He **explained** that **two years before their** management **had taken** the decision to invest in the launch of environmentally sound packaging solutions. **Their** packaging supplier **had been instructed** to use the best sustainable, recyclable and at the same time food-safe alternative. The manager **continued** that **that** change-over **had been completed the year before**. So all BIG BURGER packaging **was** plant-based and biodegradable. Holstein **emphasized** that **that** change in the manufacturing process **did not affect** the quality of the packaging.

24 1 He **emphasized the fact** that rain forest destruction **threatened** the well-being of the environment.
2 He **made it clear** that BIG BURGER **had** no part in it.
3 He **said** that nowhere in the world **did** BIG BURGER's use of beef threaten the tropical rain forest.
4 He **said** that the company **would continue to adapt** policies and practices which **were** necessary to protect the global environment.

5 He **explained** that **they were researching**/that **that included research-ing** ways of saving resources such as fossil fuels and water when producing meat and that they **were investing** in methods to minimize air and water pollution.

6 He **knew** that recycling **had become** a vital part of effective waste manage-ment because it **provided** a way to eliminate items from the waste stream.

7 He **pointed out** that BIG BURGER **was** already the largest user of biodegra-dable and recyclable packaging material in the quick service restaurant in-dustry.

8 He **said they were** currently **running** pilot schemes at several restaurants in the Croydon area.

9 He **told us** that customers **were asked to separate** their waste and put food remains in one bin and recyclable cartons in another.

10 He **stressed the fact** that a similar scheme already **operated** successfully in many of **their** US restaurants.

11 He **pointed out** that **they would continue** to ensure that **they were serving their** customers in the best and safest way while keeping environ-mental impact as low as possible.

25 Marie-Ann Winford **told** the nutritional expert (that) **she had come** to **her** for help. Marie-Ann **thought she was** too fat. She **said she didn't want to look** like a model, but **she wanted to lose** about three stone and **get** back to the weight **she had been** when **she had married**. Marie-Ann **told** the expert that the trouble **was, she lacked** will-power. **She had tried** everything, from calorie-counting to appetite suppressants. But nothing **helped. She started** a diet, but a few days later, **she would crave** for a bar of chocolate or a handful of biscuits, and it all **went** downhill again.
Marie-Ann **added she couldn't keep** anything in the house that **might tempt her** – so the whole family **was** on a diet, too, whether they **liked** it or not. **Her** husband, Anthony, and **her** children all **ate** the same food as **she**: sal-ads, low-calorie soup, low-fat spreads, diet lemonade and skimmed milk.
Only **the day before her** husband **had said he liked her** the way **she was**. But **she** sometimes **wished** he'd give **her** more encouragement. Marie-Ann **made it clear** that it **took** such a lot of effort to lose just a few pounds. She **thought he should support her** a little more. But no! **The week before** he **had brought** home a box of chocolates. Within half an hour **she had eaten** the lot. Marie-Ann **admitted she had been** thoroughly miserable and **had blamed** him – he **knew she couldn't resist** sweets when they were in front of **her**. She **wanted to know** what **she could** do.

26 1 … how long I/we had been married."
    2 … how old my/our children were."
    3 … if/whether I went to work."
    4 … what I had done before I had got married."
    5 … why I wanted to lose weight."
    6 … when I had first put on weight."
    7 … what food I liked best."
    8 … if/whether I ate in between meals."
    9 … when I ate my last meal of the day."
    10 … if/whether I had any financial worries."
    11 … if/whether I would go back to work when my/our children were older."
    12 … if/whether my/our children complained about 'health food'."
    13 … if/whether they were allowed to eat sweets in between meals.

27 1 … to eat enough of the right food."
    2 … to take up exercise every day."
    3 … to avoid eating too much fat."
    4 … to cook vegetables carefully."
    5 … not to buy any sweets."
    6 … to eat lots of fresh fruit."
    7 … to drink plenty of water."
    8 … to keep away from the fridge."
    9 … to eat a plate of raw vegetables every day."
    10 … to avoid artificially coloured and flavoured food."
    11 … not to teach my/our children unhealthy eating habits."
    12 … not to worry about my/our children's and my husband's/your weight."
    13 … to replace white flour and white rice with whole-grain products."

Der Infinitiv • The Infinitive

28 1 more and more parents decide / 2 the headmaster to register /
3 rich parents to choose / 4 employers hire / 5 their son to go /
6 her husband to reconsider / 7 young pupils hate / 8 our boy, child enjoy /
9 our boy, child to leave / 10 his wife to oppose

29 1 to get ahead / 2 to update / 3 to go / 4 to participate / 5 to take /
6 to improve / 7 to attend / 8 to prepare / 9 (to) write / 10 know /
11 meeting, meet / 12 to sit / 13 to prove / 14 to obtain

30 1 to be changed / 2 to have been asked / 3 to be asked / 4 be taught /
5 to be changed / 6 to be taught / 7 to be made to learn / 8 to facilitate /
9 to be found / 10 to be desired / 11 to adapt / 12 to teach / 13 to learn /
14 to decide / 15 to remain / 16 to cope / 17 to have

31 1 had her name put down / 2 have the skills of the staff updated /
3 made, let, had Muriel attend / 4 let her go home / 5 make her take /
6 let anybody start / 7 let you know / 8 makes his students read /
9 makes them write / 10 make anybody take / 11 lets everybody decide

32 1 Da nur noch drei Monate Zeit waren bis zur Prüfung, war Joshua ziemlich
nervös.
2 Mit der ganzen Wiederholungsarbeit, die er zu bewältigen hatte, hatte er
viel zu tun.
3 Sein Vater dachte, sein Sohn würde sich ein bisschen verloren /allein
gelassen fühlen, wenn er niemanden hätte, der ihn unterstützte; deshalb
bat er Mr Dewy, den alten Englischlehrer, Joshua zu helfen.
4 Joshuas Mutter war überzeugt, dass er es nicht schaffen würde, wenn ihm
niemand helfen würde.
5 Mr Ellis hoffte, dass Joshua hart arbeiten würde, da /wenn ihn keine
Gedanken an Ferien ablenken würden von /bei seinen Anstrengungen.
6 Für die nächsten paar Monate wird Joshua also kein Schüler sein, der
nichts zu tun hat. Im Gegenteil.
7 Wenn Joshua zusätzliche Nachhilfestunden nähme, hätte er eine größere
Chance, die Aufnahmeprüfung zu bestehen, als die meisten seiner Mit-
schüler, die niemanden haben, der ihnen hilft.

33 1 Sie hoffen sehr, dass ihr Sohn in Winchester aufgenommen wird.
2 Es ist wichtig, dass Joshua bis Juni fertig (vorbereitet) ist.
3 Es ist nicht ungewöhnlich, dass das College seine Anzahl an Stipendien er-
höht.
4 Es ist für die (Erhaltung der) Unterrichtsqualität in Winchester unbedingt
erforderlich, dass die besten Lehrer, die es gibt, dort unterrichten.

34 1   Many examination questions were too difficult **for Lisa to answer**.
2   One question was extremely difficult **for anybody to answer**.
3   It would be good **for Lisa to work** harder.
4   It's time **for her to start** today.
5   Her English essay was not good enough **for her teacher to accept** it.

35 1 unusual for Daniel to try out / 2 wait for Ron to wake up / 3 nerve-racking for the boys to watch / 4 impossible for his mates to make / 5 arrange for the janitor to come / 6 for them to do / 7 for the janitor to arrive / 8 to arrange for his father to come

Die Partizipien • The Participles

36 1 Adjektiv / 2 Gerundium / 3 Gerundium / 4 Adjektiv / 5 Partizipialkonstruktion anstelle eines Relativsatzes / 6 Gerundium / 7 Gerundium (Substantiv = Warteliste; ähnlich: *living room*) / 8 Verlaufsform / 9 Verlaufsform / 10 Gerundium

37 1 bordering / 2 doing / 3 comprising / 4 Passing mostly through rural areas cyclist must be / 5 suiting / 6 opened / 7 confirming / 8 Planned … the route / 9 running / 10 interested / 11 lying / 12 Planning National Route 1, the authorities saw to it / 13 passing / 14 wishing / 15 connecting / 16 looking / 17 using

38 1 As they felt / 2 which is based / 3 who booked / 4 which were placed / 5 As they offered   6 which were sold / 7 which last / 8 which were taken / 9 which were spent / 10 As, When they compared / 11 who holidayed / 12 which comprises / 13 who spend

39 1 Having evaluated / 2 Having visited / 3 having had / 4 Having examined / 5 sitting / 6 Having allowed / 7 Having driven / 8 Causing / 9 Doing / 10 Announcing

40 1   …, I left my London Transport Travelcard in the hotel.
2   …, I dropped my tourist map into the water.
3   …, the tourists could admire the Crown Jewels in their beauty and splendour.
4   …, you can see parts of the City of London.

5 …, I noticed / realized that my suitcase had already been taken to Gatwick Airport.
6 …, I saw the 211-bus driving past.
7 …, I saw the late-night bus coming up the road.

41 1 With especially environmentalists criticizing …
2 With fuel costs rising …
3 With so many holiday-makers flying …
4 With the Tourist Board setting up / having set up …
5 With their many exchange programmes offered …
6 With travel costs going / having gone up …
7 With demonstrators blocking …
8 With more and more computers carrying out …

42 1 Tausende von Autos fahren jeden Tag durch das Stadtzentrum und stoßen ihre dreckigen und giftigen Abgase aus.
2 Da Hunderte von lauten Lastwagen durch das Stadtzentrum fahren, befürchten die Ladenbesitzer, dass sie Kunden verlieren werden.
3 Da die Benzinpreise fast täglich steigen, müssen sparsamere Motoren entwickelt werden.
4 Mary fuhr durch den heftigen Regen, während die Scheibenwischer sich schnell von links nach rechts bewegten.
5 Da immer mehr Autos unsere Straßen verstopfen, hat die Polizei Videokameras installiert, um den Verkehrsfluss zu beobachten.
6 Weil so viele junge Fahrer Alkohol trinken und dann fahren, sind strengere Kontrollen nötig, besonders freitag- und samstagnachts.

Das Passiv • The Passive

43 1 In the sixties the removal of quotas between member countries **was agreed to** by the six founder nations.
2 Even then the slow-down in the further integration of the community **was complained about** by many politicians.
3 A joint European foreign policy **was talked about** by Pro-Europeans.
4 The ambitious plans of a "European union" **were laughed about** by Anti-Europeans.
5 The introduction of a truly free and open market **was worked on** by Delors and his collaborators in Brussels.

6   The support from influential managers **can be relied on** by the EU commission.
7   The advantages of a competitive European community **are spoken about** by businessmen in Europe.

44 1   Robert Schuman **will always be remembered** for his continuous work towards European integration by Pro-Europeans.
2   In 1973, the European community **was joined** by the former EFTA members.
3   Critics of a greater EU **shouldn't be believed**.
4   The commission in Brussels **is trusted to find** a fair compromise on controversial issues by most politicians.
5   The Queen **was met** by representatives of all parties after her address to the European parliament in Strasbourg.
6   The example of the Danes who in their majority voted for an extension of the EU **ought to be followed**.
7   Managers **will be helped to improve** trading opportunities by the knowledge of foreign languages.
8   Employees **have been ordered** by international companies to take part in a language training programme.
9   Students **are advised** by businessmen to learn at least three modern languages.

45 1   For years British companies **have been told to train** their employees in foreign language skills by foreign language teachers.
2   It is true that French **is taught** by (at) most schools in Britain, but a French menu **can be read** by only one in three people.
3   The Britons' ability to speak and understand French **is regarded** as rather modest by foreign language teachers.
4   Languages **are dropped** altogether at 14 by a large number of school leavers.
5   The view **is held** by most Britons that foreign languages **are not needed** because English **is spoken** by everybody on the Continent anyway.
6   A relationship between foreign language ability and export performance **is being shown** by recent research studies.
7   Languages **are needed** not only by managers but also by secretaries, telephonists and receptionists.

8 Market research on the Continent **will have to be done** especially by small firms.

9 A considerable increase in sales **has been achieved** by companies with multilingual employees.

46 1 All countries **are forced to upgrade** their environmental protection standards by the EU commission.

2 Community standards for water quality **are met** by more British beaches.

3 Untreated sewage **is** still **being poured** into lakes and rivers by many cities.

4 Stricter limits on pollution from car exhausts **are being introduced** by all EU countries.

5 The pollution from chimneys **will have to be reduced** by coal-fired power stations.

6 The effect a new motorway will have on the environment **has to be taken** into consideration by planners.

7 Before the first brick **can be laid** (by the builders) the impact of the new factory on humans, flora and fauna **must be studied** by architects.

8 All countries **are encouraged to raise** their environmental standards by the EU.

9 All nations **are expected to contribute** to a cleaner and healthier air in Europe.

10 It is hoped that all trespassers of the new regulations **will be prosecuted** (by the police).

47 1 The enlargement of the European Union **is said to be** a sensible move.

2 An extended EU **is believed to enhance** the security of all its members.

3 The enlarged EU **is acknowledged to boost** economic growth.

4 The new EU **is claimed to provide** a better quality of life for citizens throughout Europe.

5 Stricter EU policies **are expected to help** create a cleaner environment.

6 The arrival of new members **is presumed to enrich** the EU's cultural diversity.

7 Customs controls **are thought to be** a waste of time.

8 Air travel **is known to be** less expensive than it used to be.

9 Airlines **are said to be** free to fly the routes they want.

10 Restrictive practices between airlines **are reported to be** illegal.

48 1 have been drawn up / 2 have been developed / 3 were discussed / 4 (were) rejected / 5 was signed / 6 was to be built / 7 were not laid down / 8 had to be paid for / 9 were flooded / 10 was to be financed / 11 was won / 12 to be dug / 13 were raised / 14 could only be expected / 15 was given / 16 was troubled / 17 had to be invested / 18 was nicknamed / 19 had to be overcome / 20 would be trapped / 21 could easily be attacked / 22 would be driven / 23 would be lost / 24 would be destroyed / 25 was organized / 26 was informed / 27 was built / 28 was achieved / 29 were employed / 30 were killed / 31 were questioned / 32 were better trained / 33 have been proved / 34 has been kept / 35 to be solved / 36 was built / 37 had to be covered / 38 was opened / 39 has been reduced

Präpositionen • Prepositions

49 1 The Eurostar train service operates **between** Brussels and London.
2 The Isle of Man lies **in** the Irish Sea.
3 Ferries sail **from** Liverpool **to** Dublin.
4 Bristol can be reached **on** the M4.
5 Leeds lies **in** Yorkshire.
6 Blackpool is a famous resort **by** the sea.
7 The distance **between** London and Sheffield is 166 miles.
8 The Eurostar tunnel is **under** the English Channel.
9 International companies drill for oil **off** the coast of Scotland.
10 The London Eye towers **above/over** the Houses of Parliament.

50 1 on / 2 in / 3 into / 4 of / 5 of / 6 to / 7 From / 8 at / 9 at / 10 with / 11 with / 12 through / 13 at / 14 to / 15 of / 16 by / 17 of / 18 with / 19 for / 20 from / 21 of / 22 from / 23 about / 24 from / 25 to / 26 with / 27 for / 28 through / 29 on / 30 between / 31 at / 32 to / 33 in, of / 34 towards / 35 from / 36 from / 37 on

51 1 at / 2 around / 3 in / 4 with / 5 in / 6 up / 7 in / 8 between / 9 in / 10 At / 11 in / 12 on / 13 in

52 Hello Ron and Geraldine,

Thanks for inviting me to come **to** America!

I've just received confirmation of the flights which I've booked to visit you **over** the Christmas holidays and would like to tell you how I'll get **to** Boston and back home again **in** the New Year.

As direct flights are expensive I have booked cheaper flights via London and Chicago (for my journey home). I don't mind changing planes.

I'll leave Frankfurt **on** Friday, December 23 **at** 7:45 **in** the morning, arriving **in** London Heathrow **at** 8:35. **At** 10:30 American Airlines flight No. 109 will take me **to** Boston where I will arrive **at** 12:50 **in** the afternoon. Hopefully there is no delay and I will be able to meet you then.

The details of my return flight are as follows: **On** January 6 (which is a Sunday) I'll take American Airlines flight No. 2003 scheduled **at** 3:29 **in** the afternoon to take me **to** Chicago. **In** the evening of the same day **at** 7:30 American Airlines flight No. 84 will fly me home **to** Frankfurt, where I will arrive **on** the following day (Monday) **at** 12:10 **in** the afternoon. My parents and brother will pick me up.

I'm looking forward very much to seeing you again! I'll skype with Vanessa today or tomorrow.

Best wishes,

Christina

53 1 in / 2 at / 3 with / 4 In / 5 to / 6 from / 7 in / 8 of / 9 In / 10 through / 11 below / 12 of / 13 at / 14 In / 15 to / 16 through / 17 on / 18 at / 19 in, on / 20 on / 21 in / 22 into / 23 down / 24 from

54 1 of / 2 In / 3 on / 4 in / 5 for / 6 During / 7 into / 8 up / 9 in / 10 to / 11 from / 12 in / 13 at / 14 at / 15 in / 16 on / 17 for / 18 at / 19 into / 20 on

Relativpronomen • Relative Pronouns

55 1   h   broadsheet = expression **which** is used for the quality papers, referring to the size of the paper used for printing

    2   f   colour supplement = free magazine **which** is included in the normal Sunday paper, carrying lots of advertisements

    3   l   correspondent = journalist **who** writes for one or more papers, mainly from abroad

4 　e　 editor-in-chief = journalist **who** is in charge of the publication of a paper

5 　b　 gossip column = section in a newspaper **which** covers "news" about the lives of famous people

6 　d　 "heavy" = nickname **which** is applied to the more serious newspapers (e. g. "The Times")

7 　g　 national newspaper = a newspaper **which** is read all over the country (e. g. "The Guardian")

8 　j　 page-three-girl = young model **whose** picture is printed in a tabloid, mostly in a topless pose

9 　k　 publishing house = a company **which** produces newspapers, magazines and books

10 　c　 sponsor (of a TV programme) = a company **which** finances a TV programme, e. g. a soap opera

11 　a　 tabloid = a newspaper **which** caters for the taste of the masses (e. g. "The Sun")

12 　i　 tycoon = someone **who** owns several papers, radio and TV stations

56 1 who / 2 whose / 3 what / 4 who / 5 whom / 6 which / 7 which / 8 which / 9 What / 10 which / 11 who / 12 that / 13 which / 14 that / 15 What / 16 which / 17 which / 18 which / 19 which / 20 whose / 21 which / 22 who / 23 who / 24 which / 25 What

57 1 The early American soap operas on television, which were developed in the sixties, were daytime serials, which were created to transport advertisements for housewives. (non-defining)

2 The scripts which are written for the most successful BBC series "East Enders" have become more realistic. (defining)

3 Most TV critics agree that the BBC soap "East Enders" is a drama series which – more or less – reflects society accurately. (defining)

4 Today's American soaps show male characters who are often macho and tyrannical. (defining)

5 A character to fit this description is J. R., who appeared in "Dallas". (non-defining)

6 The new Director-General of the BBC, who took over from his predecessor last week, announced a change in the company's programme strategy. (non-defining)

7 He said the BBC would remain a company which offers programmes for everybody. (defining)

8 But the company would not follow the example of private broadcasters who try to attract a larger audience with ever "cheaper" – which means sillier – programmes. (defining)

9 American or Australian soaps like "Neighbours", which brought fame to Kylie Minogue, would no longer be shown on BBC. (non-defining)

58 1 Charles Schultz's cartoon strip, **which** has been translated into more than 60 languages, is still known all over the world.

2 The final name of the strip, **whose** original title was "Li'l Folks", was "Peanuts".

3 In the early days newspaper readers, most of **whom** were not used to the new kind of humour, didn't like the strips very much.

4 But the "Peanuts", **whose** readership included people of every social standing, became very popular.

5 During the 1960s a profitable merchandising industry was developed **which** sold for example Charlie Brown clocks and Snoopy soft toys.

6 The strip's main character is Charlie Brown, **who** has won the hearts of millions of readers.

7 Charlie represents the typical loser **who** can never win the girl he loves. / Charlie, **who** represents the typical loser, can never win the girl he loves.

8 A girl **whose** name is Lucy makes Charlie's life really miserable.

9 Charlie is popular with only few members of the "Peanuts" gang, one of **whom** is Peppermint Patty.

10 The death of Charles Schulz, **which** occurred in 2000, ended the run of the "Peanuts".

Zeiten • Tenses

59 1 have always played / 2 experienced / 3 needed / 4 underwent / 5 had been / 6 was then turned / 7 sought / 8 relied / 9 could be served / 10 could also be used / 11 emerged / 12 brought / 13 led / 14 struck / 15 are known / 16 did not solve / 17 has not changed / 18 rose / 19 had to / 20 came / 21 passed / 22 have been, were set up

60 1 has been / 2 have always had / 3 colonized / 4 arrived / 5 are looking back / 6 was divided / 7 chose / 8 became / 9 declared / 10 has existed / 11 faces / 12 represent / 13 are / 14 seem unable / 15 give / 16 commemorate / 17 wear / 18 is condemned

61 1 joined / 2 was / 3 was / 4 had / 5 were / 6 was / 7 reduced / 8 were /
9 could be counted / 10 were aged / 11 had survived / 12 were / 13 had gone /
14 were / 15 could find / 16 came / 17 improved / 18 joined / 19 benefited /
20 received / 21 was invested / 22 facilitated / 23 experienced /
24 was often referred to / 25 (had) emigrated / 26 came / 27 ended /
28 have been made / 29 was nicknamed / 30 (has) also brought /
31 was improved / 32 have come / 33 fight, are fighting

62 1 have been tearing/have torn / 2 for / 3 Since / 4 have dominated / 5 Since /
6 have improved; have been improving / 7 have been intensified / 8 for /
9 For / 10 has been / 11 for / 12 has been replaced / 13 has attracted, has been
attracting / 14 since / 15 have grown / 16 since / 17 has steadily increased,
has been steadily increasing / 18 for / 19 have never looked / 20 since

63 1 has not always been / 2 have experienced / 3 have touched / 4 (have) been
injured / 5 had been done / 6 could have imagined / 7 have done / 8 set /
9 have also shed / 10 would be standing / 11 were / 12 was painstakingly
loosened / 13 were / 14 have now come / 15 voted / 16 will prevail

64 1 rolled / 2 has changed / 3 supplied / 4 has become / 5 chose /
6 has remained / 7 has long since disappeared / 8 prospered / 9 declared /
10 spread / 11 carried / 12 has always been / 13 was founded / 14 has been /
15 has been

Tests

Test 1   Changing Places

1   Guillaume said, "I am interested in playing with computers and I don't like
sport."

2   a)   Having celebrated / after celebrating my 13th birthday I played host to
a 15-year-old French girl for a month.

b)   What the people providing you with Camille or Lukas for three weeks
of the summer holiday do not tell you is that the outcome is dictated
by luck.

3   Luck dictates the outcome.

4   People think / It is said / thought / believed that foreign exchanges widen
horizons.

5 non-defining relative clause giving additional information; can be omitted, is marked off by commas

6 If Agnes hadn't come from a big city she wouldn't have hated rural Devon.

7 a) lasting – adjective
   b) speaking – connection (= and speak)
   c) playing – gerund (after preposition)
   d) eating – predicative complement (= part of the predicate)

8 Foreign languages are being used by young children.

9 Guillaume said (that) he liked eating toast at lunchtime and (that) he was extremely pleased about having everything on the same plate at dinner.

Test 2 Homeless Teenagers

1 of, in, among, in, in, on, in, with, in

2 a) The diaries reflect an existence which is dominated by lack of money.
   b) The plight of the young homeless is illustrated by the publication of extracts from the diaries of more than 100 youngsters who were asked by Shelter.

3 The publication of extracts from the diaries of more than 100 youngsters illustrates the plight of the young homeless.

4 a) Housing prospects for the young homeless have been reduced by recent legislation.
   b) The Government is being called on by Shelter to take immediate action.

5 She said (that) to the vast majority of young people who contacted them, that change wouldn't make a scrap of difference because the extra benefit was only payable for 12 to 16 weeks.

6 a) growing – adjective
   wandering – participle construction instead of a relative clause
   b) calling – continuous /progressive form
   c) overcrowding – noun, gerund
   d) moving + begging – gerunds after prepositions

7 are / is steadily growing / estimates / are / will rise / leave / have been / has added

8 The homeless charity Shelter estimates that nationally there are 150,000 homeless young people, 30,000 of whom are in London.

9 which / who / what / who / that / what / whose / – / which

10 to leave / to look / talking / of going / of having / watching / of listening to / turning / in sharing / of leaving / of joining / to talk

Test 3   Are You Eating the Right Kind of Food?

1   in / from / of / for / in / of / of

2   a)   Carbohydrates, which may be converted into body fat, provide the body with energy.

     b)   Fats, which may also form body fat, provide energy in a more concentrated form than carbohydrates.

     c)   Vitamins, most of which help to regulate body processes, are essential.

3   It is important for adolescents to satisfy their appetites with well-balanced meals.

4   The expert said (that) obesity among schoolchildren was then (at that time) probably one of the commonest forms of malnutrition and that (that) might continue into adult life. He added (that) there was some evidence that adolescent obesity might be partly due to the general decrease of physical activity.

5   a)   Sweet and sticky foods and snacks which are eaten between meals are one cause of dental decay.

     b)   Cranky diets which are based on one or two foods only are rarely successful.

6   defining (necessary) relative clause – not marked off by commas

7   A knowledge of nutrition will be beneficial to the health of young people for the rest of their lives.

8   The energy intake should be cut down to about 1,000 kilocalories each day (by slimmers).

9   People/slimmers/people on a diet should include breakfast into any diet plan.

10   a)   Eating – progressive/continuous form

     b)   living – adjective

     c)   eating – participle construction instead of a relative clause

     d)   slimming – adjective/gerund (noun)

11   Passive infinitive

Jetzt mal **BUTTER** bei die Fische.

Feedback

Liebe Kundin, lieber Kunde,

der STARK Verlag hat das Ziel, Sie effektiv beim Lernen zu unterstützen. In welchem Maße uns dies gelingt, wissen Sie am besten. Deshalb bitten wir Sie, uns Ihre Meinung zu den STARK-Produkten in dieser Umfrage mitzuteilen:

www.stark-verlag.de/feedback

Als Dankeschön verlosen wir einmal jährlich, zum 31. Juli, unter allen Teilnehmern ein aktuelles Samsung-Tablet. Für nähere Informationen und die Teilnahmebedingungen folgen Sie dem Internetlink.

Herzlichen Dank!

Haben Sie weitere Fragen an uns?
Sie erreichen uns telefonisch **0180 3 179000***
per E-Mail **info@stark-verlag.de**
oder im Internet unter **www.stark-verlag.de**

Lernen▪Wissen▪Zukunft
STARK

*9 Cent pro Min. aus dem deutschen Festnetz, Mobilfunk bis 42 Cent pro Min. Aus dem Mobilfunknetz wählen Sie die Festnetznummer: **08167 9573-0**

Erfolgreich durchs Abitur mit den **STARK** Reihen

Abiturprüfung

Anhand von Original-Auf-
gaben die Prüfungssituation
trainieren. Schülergerechte
Lösungen helfen bei der
Leistungskontrolle.

Abitur-Training

Prüfungsrelevantes Wissen
schülergerecht präsentiert.
Übungsaufgaben mit
Lösungen sichern den
Lernerfolg.

Klausuren

Durch gezieltes Klausuren-
training die Grundlagen
schaffen für eine gute
Abinote.

Kompakt-Wissen

Kompakte Darstellung des
prüfungsrelevanten Wissens
zum schnellen Nachschlagen
und Wiederholen.

Interpretationen

Perfekte Hilfe beim
Verständnis literarischer
Werke.

Und vieles mehr auf
www.stark-verlag.de